Creating COMPETITIVE Power Markets:
the PJM Model

Creating
COMPETITIVE
Power Markets:
the PJM Model

Jeremiah D. Lambert

Copyright© 2001 by
PennWell Corporation
1421 S. Sheridan Road
Tulsa, Oklahoma 74112
800-752-9764
sales@pennwell.com
www.pennwell-store.com
www.pennwell.com

cover and book design by Amy Spehar

Library of Congress Cataloging-in-Publication Data

Lambert, Jeremiah D., 1934-
    Creating competitive markets : the PJM model / Jeremiah D. Lambert.
        p. cm.
    Includes bibliographical references and index.
    ISBN 0-87814-791-8
        1. Electric utilities--Middle Atlantic States--Management. I. title.
HD9685.U6 M4758 2001
333.793'217'0975--dc21

Printed in the United States of America.

1   2   3   4   5   05   04   03   02   01

Dedication

To Sanda, with love

$\mathcal{T}$able of Contents

List of Figures

*L*ist of Tables

List of Acronyms

ACE	area control error
ACES	accounting contracts and energy schedules
AFUDC	allowance for funds used during construction
ALM	active load management
APS	Allegheny Power System
AR	area regulation
ATC	available transmission capacity
BG&E	Baltimore Gas & Electric
CBM	capacity benefit margin
COB	California-Oregon border
CT	combustion turbine
DRA	Dispute Resolution Agreement
ECAR	East Central Area Reliability Council
eDART	Dispatcher application and reporting tool
eData	PJM electronic data
EEES	Electric Electronic Engineering Society
EFORd	demand equivalent forced outage rate
eGADS	Generator Availability Data System
EHV	extra high voltage
eMKT	Website allowing PJM market participants to submit generation offer data, demand bid, increments offers, decrement bids, and regulation offers into the market's database.
EMS	Energy Management System
EPAct	Energy Policy Act of 1992
ERCOT	Electric Reliability Council of Texas
FCITC	first contingency incremental transfer capability
FCTTC	first contingency total transfer capability
FERC	Federal Energy Regulatory Commission
FPA	Federal Power Act
FRCC	Florida Reliability Coordinating Council
FTR	fixed transmission rights
GPU	General Public Utilities
GWHR	gigawatt hour
Hz	hertz
IPP	independent power producer

ISA	interconnection service agreement
ISO	independent system operator
ISOA	Independent system operator agreement
kV	kilovolt
LA	load aggregator
LDC	local distribution company
LFUM	load forecast uncertainty margin
LLC	limited liability company
LMP	locational marginal price
LPA	locational price algorithm module
LSE	load serving entities
MAAC	Mid-Atlantic Area Council
MAIN	Mid-America Interconnected Network
MAPP	Mid-Continent Area Power Pool
MMP	market monitoring plan
MMU	market monitoring unit
MOA	Market Operations Agreement
MUI	market user interface
MVAR	megavar
MW	megawatt
MWh	megawatt hour
NAPSIC	North American Power System Interconnection Committee
NEPEX	New England Power Exchange
NEPOOL	New England Power Pool
NERC	North American Electric Reliability Council
NJPIRG	New Jersey Public Interest Research Group
NOM	normal operating margin
NPCC	Northeast Power Coordinating Council
NYISO	New York Independent System Operator
NYPP	New York Power Pool
OA	operating agreement
OASIS	open access same-time information system
OC	off-cost
OI	office of the interconnection

PA-NJ	Pennsylvania-New Jersey
PECO	Philadelphia Electric Company
PEPCO	Potomac Electric Power Company
PICS	PJM import capability study
PJM	Pennsylvania-New Jersey-Maryland
PJMIA	PJM Interconnection Association
PJMnet	PJM's intranet
PP&L	Pennsylvania Power & Light
PSE&G	Public Service Electric & Gas
PUHCA	Public Utility Holding Company Act of 1935
PURPA	Public Utility Regulatory Policy Act of 1978
PX	PJM interchange energy market
RAA	reliability assurance agreement
RSA	Reserve Sharing Agreement
RTEP	regional transmission expansion plan
RTO	regional transmission organization
SCADA	supervisory control and data acquisition
SERC	Southeastern Electric Reliability Council
SFT	simultaneous feasibility test
SPP	Southwestern Power Pool
TLR	transmission loading relief
TMI	Three Mile Island
TOA	transmission owners agreement
transco	transmission company
TRM	transmission reliability margin
TTC	total transfer capability
TVA	Tennessee Valley Authority
ULFM	unanticipated loop flow margin
VaPwr	Virginia Power
WSCC	Western Systems Coordinating Council

Acknowledgements

When a busy lawyer undertakes a literary frolic and detour, he needs the goodwill and encouragement of his colleagues. My partners at Shook, Hardy & Bacon LLP have offered both, not to mention resources, patience, and forbearance, for which the author is duly appreciative.

My longtime secretary and administrative assistant, Cynthia King, has provided invaluable assistance with data retrieval, paper flow, and the myriad clerical details involved in producing a technical book.

Curtis D. Blanc, an associate in the Washington, D.C. office of the firm, has assisted ably and indefatigably with the diverse research tasks and editorial support required in an effort of this kind.

Neil Dyson, a paralegal in the Washington, D.C. office of the firm, has efficiently run to ground numerous cases, obscure monographs, and regulatory filings.

Jeff Williams of PJM Interconnection LLC has served as the author's bridge to the subject of this book, ever ready, willing and able to provide necessary materials, feedback, and critical judgment.

Not least, the author's spouse, Sanda Lambert, has without complaint accommodated this book's intrusion into domestic life and offered her loyal support.

To all of the above, my grateful thanks.

Jeremiah D. Lambert
Washington, D.C.
July 2001

Foreword

As the consequences of California's flawed electricity deregulation scheme continue to unfold, policymakers nationwide have expressed concern about restructuring of the electric power industry. In the current climate of uncertainty and retrenchment, however, California is not the only benchmark for electric power restructuring.

The indicative competitive model is instead the market operated by PJM, which succeeds where California fails.

PJM has operated successfully since 1997; implemented innovative and functional business rules; produced reasonable prices; matched growing demand with new investment, and put in place the nation's most liquid energy trading market.

PJM's market operates on a balancing and day-ahead basis; provides sellers and buyers the opportunity to trade through spot transactions or bilateral agreements, and has made increasing use of innovative technologies, allowing participants to do business in real time pursuant to a transparent Internet-based regime. PJM at the same time manages a single control area that is a paragon of reliability.

PJM has expanded its mid-Atlantic footprint through the formation of PJM West, with Allegheny Power. It has exported its business rules and system software to other markets. Most significantly, PJM is now recognized by FERC as the regional transmission organization of choice for the entire Northeast.

In this book I seek to explain how PJM works and how, through astute and technically oriented management, it has become a state-of-the-art, knowledge-based instrument for transformation of the electric power industry.

Jeremiah D. Lambert
Washington, D.C.
July 2001

CHAPTER ONE

The Road to Competitive Electric Markets

Federal Regulatory Initiatives

In their landmark study, *Markets for Power,* Paul L. Joskow and Richard Schmalensee, writing in 1983, forecast the structure of the deregulated power industry in the United States. As read in a contemporary context, the authors' vision proves remarkably prescient. In one scenario, they assume transfer of ownership and operation of all high-voltage transmission lines to a "regional power pooling and transmission entity" with no interest in generation.

Under this scenario, linkages between distribution, transmission, and generation occur across markets—regulated and unregulated—rather than through internal organization.

Market forces call forth appropriate quantities and types of generating capacity. Actual physical delivery of power, however, always takes place through a real-time pooling-transmission entity subject to agreements to dispatch plants, make financial settlements, and provide for transmission and resale of power.[1]

So described, Joskow's and Schmalensee's transmission entity has the salient characteristics of the independent system operator (ISO) that, almost 20 years later, has become the centerpiece of the Federal Energy Regulatory Commission's (FERC) ongoing initiative to restructure the nation's electric power industry.

Emergence of competitive markets

The intervening decades, as foreseen, have witnessed relentless change. Competitive markets have emerged in wholesale and retail electric power, now routinely traded as a commodity. Vertically integrated investor-owned utilities have in many instances exited generation and/or transmission businesses. Once the providers of bundled energy service at regulated cost-based rates, they now offer or pay market-based prices for wholesale power, no longer protected by exclusive territorial franchises. In the last five years power marketers and wholesale customers have facilitated growth of short-term spot markets in electric power, using financial instruments to hedge risk. Customers now also can choose suppliers, in both wholesale and (increasingly) retail markets. Not least, the architecture of the industry itself is being regionalized and transformed into coherent submarkets, each dependent on a regional transmission organization (RTO), which, in theory at least, may be an ISO, a grid company, or a transmission company (transco).

The critical interaction in power market design is between transmission and dispatch. In an electric power grid, control of dispatch is the only way in which use of the network can be adjusted and true marginal prices determined. Open and nondiscriminatory access to the grid therefore requires open access to unbiased dispatch through a system operator who coordinates use of the transmission system and yet is independent of market participants. As developed and refined in markets such as PJM, short-run market design typically includes the following elements:

- an appropriate system operator to coordinate the short-term spot market through bid-based, security-constrained economic dispatch
- market-clearing locational marginal prices, nodal rather than zonal, reflecting congestion costs and system losses
- bilateral transactions with system-imposed network usage charges consistent with congestion pricing
- a two-settlement system with financially binding day-ahead markets, followed by real-time balancing at real-time locational marginal prices
- fixed transmission rights to allow trading of congestion hedges
- establishment of prices and performance standards for unbundled ancillary services

Globally, competitive markets have emerged along these lines within the last decade, following privatization of state-owned electric power monopolies. Apart from those in the United States, power pools now function (among other venues) in England and Wales, Australia, Canada, Norway, and Sweden. Such pools have unbundled the electricity supply industry into component parts consisting of generation, a wholesale market, transmission, distribution, and power retailing. In England and Wales power retailing until recently involved buying from the pool (through which all wholesale electricity flowed), hedging volatility with financial contracts for differences, and selling to end-use customers. Under new electricity trading arrangements initiated in 2000 to replace the pool bulk electricity is traded forward through bilateral contracts (both long- and short-term) and on power exchanges, subject to balancing and settlement cost. In Norway power retailers buy from generators pursuant to bilateral contracts and from a spot market at the margin, using futures contracts to manage risk. In both markets, customers can access the pool or spot market.[2] In each instance the pools seek to maximize competition in generation, are open to all market participants, and compete on price, not cost.[3]

Typically, a transmission system connects electricity producers and consumers over a large area in which each action by a producer or consumer can affect all market participants within the system. In the United States, for example, all states excluding Texas east of the Rocky Mountains form what is in effect a single network. System operators within that network ensure that increases in demand are met by additional generation and that unplanned outages are met by load shedding or substitute sources of generation. Historically, such load balancing has been the hallmark of power pools, *i.e.,* groups of contiguous utilities operating on a coordinated basis to achieve economies unavailable to each on a stand-alone basis.

PJM has long been regarded as the prototypical tight power pool. Even prior to becoming an ISO in 1997, PJM operated a pool-wide transmission tariff and a bid-based energy market throughout a single control area[4] comprising all or part of Pennsylvania, New Jersey, Maryland, Delaware, Virginia, and the District of Columbia. Through its control center, located near Valley Forge, Pennsylvania, PJM coordinates the operation of approximately 540 generating units encompassing more than 58,000 megawatts (MW) of installed capacity, available to supply a 14,100-mile transmission grid covering nearly 50,000 square miles. PJM's long history of effective operations, dating from 1927 and including 8 utility systems, has facilitated its transition to RTO status (Fig. 1-1).

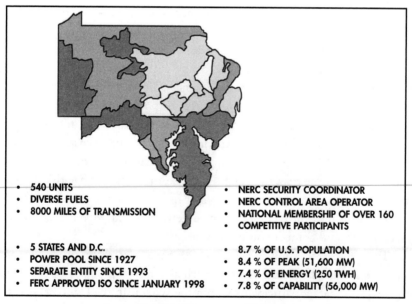

- 540 UNITS
- DIVERSE FUELS
- 8000 MILES OF TRANSMISSION

- NERC SECURITY COORDINATOR
- NERC CONTROL AREA OPERATOR
- NATIONAL MEMBERSHIP OF OVER 160
- COMPETITIVE PARTICIPANTS

- 5 STATES AND D.C.
- POWER POOL SINCE 1927
- SEPARATE ENTITY SINCE 1993
- FERC APPROVED ISO SINCE JANUARY 1998

- 8.7 % OF U.S. POPULATION
- 8.4 % OF PEAK (51,600 MW)
- 7.4 % OF ENERGY (250 TWH)
- 7.8 % OF CAPABILITY (56,000 MW)

Fig. 1-1 Overview of PJM

Since 1997 PJM has been the nation's only full-function ISO. In that capacity PJM:

- centrally schedules and dispatches the installed capacity mentioned earlier and wholesale transmission in six jurisdictions (all or portions of Delaware, Maryland, New Jersey, Pennsylvania, Virginia, and the District of Columbia) comprising 23 million end-users of electricity
- performs the functions of the North American Electric Reliability Council regional reliability area coordinator for the Mid-Atlantic Region
- operates five energy markets, including a real-time power exchange that is the most vibrant wholesale spot market for electricity in the nation
- is responsible for preparing and implementing regional transmission expansion planning
- operates a single, uniform tariff for all transmission customers[5]

Open-access transmission

The indispensable predicate for development of competitive markets is open-access, non-discriminatory transmission. Power transmission lines are classical essential facilities—a natural monopoly whose owner can, in the absence of a regulatory mandate, keep competitors out of indicated markets. If the owner is a vertically integrated utility with generation assets, its control of transmission can be used to favor its own generation at the expense of potential third-party suppliers, resulting in higher than competitive prices and other abuses.[6]

Therefore, market reform in the United States has focused on the bottleneck implications of transmission facilities owned or controlled by market participants. To encourage transmission access and enhance competition in wholesale markets, the Energy Policy Act of 1992 (EPA) gave FERC broad authority to order wheeling of power, *i.e.*, the transfer of electric power from a generator to a purchaser over the transmission system of an intermediate utility.[7]

The law removed most of the onerous native load protections, previously contained in Sections 211 and 212 of the Federal Power Act that had effectively neutralized FERC's ability to compel the transmission of power, either on its own or in response to a complaint. Before enactment of the EPA, FERC could only proceed indirectly by using unrelated powers under the Federal Power Act to cause utilities to provide transmission services, specifically its Section 203 authority to approve and condition utility mergers[8] and its Section 205 and 206 authority to set wholesale rates.[9] In *Utah Power & Light* Co.,[10] a landmark case, FERC conditioned a merger upon the participants' acceptance of broad obligations to provide transmission services to third parties—a practice that came to be known as "open access."[11] Typically, however, early open access tariffs required only that a utility provide point-to-point transmission services and did not mandate service to third parties equivalent to that which the utility itself enjoyed. Under Section 211 as amended, FERC granted requests for network service permitting the applicant to integrate load and resources on an instantaneous basis.[12]

Order No. 888

Although an important step, the EPA nonetheless constituted only a partial response. It became quickly apparent that case-by-case adjudication of transmission disputes under Section 211 could not effectively assure open access to the nation's transmission system.[13] To meet such concerns, in 1996 FERC issued Order No. 888, a broad rule stating that the "legal and policy cornerstone . . . is to remedy undue discrimination in access to the monopoly-owned transmission wires that control whether and to whom electricity can be transported in interstate commerce."[14] For this purpose FERC's principal instrument was a *pro forma* open access non-discriminatory transmission tariff containing minimum terms and conditions of service, including both network and point-to-point service. All public utilities owning interstate transmission facilities were required to file such tariffs and take service thereunder for their own wholesale sales and purchases of power. The key to non-discrimination was comparability of service.[15]

FERC ordered access pursuant to its authority over public utilities under Sections 205 and 206 of the Federal Power Act, not its authority to order case-by-case transmission under Sections 211 and 212, as amended. As a result, the open access requirement did not directly apply to non-public utilities such as municipalities, most cooperatives, and federal power marketing agencies. The *pro forma* tariff was nonetheless accessible by any person eligible to seek a Section 211 transmission order, including any investor-owned utility, municipality, cooperative, independent power producer, affiliated power producer, qualifying facility, or power marketer. Non-public utilities taking open access service from public utilities were required to offer comparable access in return but not to have an open access tariff of general applicability. The transmission provider was an eligible customer under its own tariff. Retail customers were eligible for service where utilities offered unbundled retail transmission service voluntarily or pursuant to a state requirement.

In addition to requiring that utilities file an open access tariff, Order No. 888 and Order No. 889 contemplated the functional unbundling of transmission and generation. Functional unbundling means:

- a utility must take both wholesale and unbundled retail transmission service under its own tariff
- quote separate rates for wholesale generation, transmission, and ancillary services
- develop an electronic information network that accords all users of the transmission system comparable access to transmission information
- follow a code of conduct that separates employees involved in transmission operations from those involved in wholesale marketing functions[16]

Power pools

However, mere functional unbundling was insufficient to mitigate utilities' vertical market power. For this purpose FERC sought structural separation, applied regionally and not simply to individual utilities. Order

No. 888 therefore accorded special attention to power pools and ISOs, which had been the subject of FERC technical conferences in 1995 and early 1996. Tight power pools such as PJM had long existed to aggregate and centrally dispatch the generating capacity of contiguous utilities through high voltage interconnection of systems within a region. Benefits included reductions in installed and capacity reserves, lower operating costs, and enhanced service reliability.

The economic benefits of pooling lie largely in the economies of scale and advantages of the diversities in load, risks and operating costs available among coordinating systems.[17] Investment costs are reduced through use of larger, centrally dispatched units and through reduced reserve margins, which result from lowering the ratio of generating unit size to combined system peak load. Operating economies are gained through load diversity of combined systems, reduced operating costs per unit of output of larger units, and more extensive use of lower cost generation available anywhere in the combined systems. Reliability benefits are also available through access to support from other systems, typically realized as a reduction in both operating and installed reserves required to achieve a given level of reliability. The existence of transfer capability determines the economic value of system interconnection as a means of improving reliability. There is a tradeoff between adding generating reserve capacity and installing additional transmission facilities to achieve equivalent reliability (Fig. 1-2).

To control generation and transmission, each interconnected network is divided for operating purposes into discrete control areas, each of which has a geographical and electrical boundary. A tight power pool, such as PJM, may operate a single control area. Subject to central dispatch, all generating utilities within a control area operate and control their combined resources to meet their combined loads as one system. Each control area has at least one dispatch center to monitor system generation output, system frequency, and tie line power flows within the control area and between it and contiguous control areas. The term "economic dispatch" refers to the process of operating the various resources of the system to minimize overall costs. It is a function of economic dispatch to determine the proper loading on each unit so total load is met at the lowest possible production cost consistent with other necessary

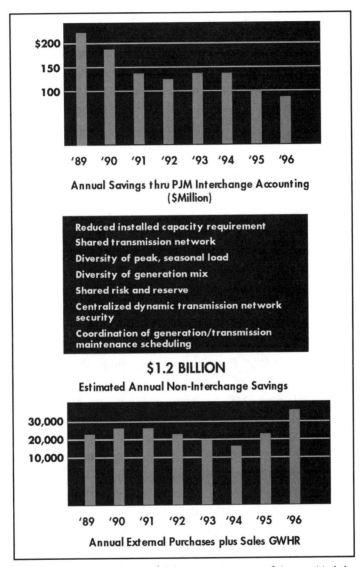

Fig. 1–2 PJM's Transfer Capability as a Function of System Viability

constraints, such as transmission line loading, transmission losses, spinning reserve requirements, and environmental considerations. [18]

In contrast to bilateral arrangements, therefore, power pools present "an intricate set of rights, obligations and considerations among [its] members. . ."[19] The filing of individual open access tariffs by constituent members of a power pool is not enough "to cure undue discrimination in transmission if those public utilities can continue to trade with a selective group within a power pool that discriminatorily excludes others from becoming a member and that provides preferential intra-pool transmission rights and rates."[20]

FERC requirements

To address this problem FERC required tight power pools such as PJM to file reformed power pooling agreements and a joint pool-wide *pro forma* tariff by December 31, 1996. Starting on that date, pool members were also required to take service under the pool-wide tariff, and the pool itself was to be open to any bulk power market participant, regardless of entity type, affiliation, or geographic location. FERC's deadline induced stakeholders in PJM to address numerous contested restructuring issues, not least the configuration of an ISO for the PJM control area.

In Order No. 888 FERC encouraged, although it did not require, the formation of ISOs to run the pool-wide transmission system. Drawing on international examples, its own transmission precedents, and a substantial body of theoretical writing, FERC viewed the ISO as an effective means of operationally unbundling vertically integrated utilities with monopoly power over territorial franchises by separating their control of transmission from ownership and control of generation and distribution. Although short of divestiture, ISO-driven operational unbundling represented a potential structural fix. The question nonetheless remained how to define the minimum necessary characteristics of an acceptable ISO, a vehicle then rooted in theory rather than practice.

Independent system operators

To provide guidance to applicants submitting ISO proposals to FERC, Order No. 888 set forth general principles of organization and operation for

ISOs as control area operators, including those established in the restructuring of power pools. Since FERC had expressly declined to mandate ISOs (none then existed in the United States), the principles were prospective in nature and designed to achieve restructuring through independent operational control of transmission (operational unbundling), not its divestiture. To this end, FERC determined:

- An ISO must be independent of any individual market participant or any class of participants (*e.g.*, transmission owners or end-users) Independence is a function of the ISO's governance structure, which could include "fair representation of all types of users of the system" on its governing board or as FERC subsequently found, a non-stakeholder board not dependent on neutralization of user classes through concurrent representation but instead on independence from all market participants and user groups. A related principle dictates that an ISO and its employees have no financial interest in the performance of any power market participant, which in turn can have no ownership interest in an ISO.
- An ISO must provide open access, self-scheduled transmission at non-pancaked rates under a single, unbundled, grid-wide tariff applicable to all eligible users in a non-discriminatory manner.
- An ISO must have primary responsibility for short-term reliability of grid operations, including planning and oversight of maintenance of transmission facilities under its control.
- An ISO must control the operation of specific transmission facilities within the system.
- An ISO must also exercise some degree of operational control over generation facilities within the system in order to regulate and balance power flows and relieve transmission constraints pursuant to established trading rules.
- An ISO must efficiently perform operational functions, such as determination of system expansion, transmission maintenance, operation of a settlements system, and operation of an energy auction.

- An ISO's transmission and ancillary services pricing policies must promote efficient use of and investment in generation, transmission, and consumption.
- An ISO must make transmission system information publicly available on a timely basis through an electronic information network, including information on system operation, available capacity, and constraints and contracts or service arrangements.
- An ISO must coordinate with neighboring control areas to ensure provision of transmission services that cross system boundaries.

These broad principles have determined the functions, structure, and governance of ISOs that have since come into being, mostly as a consequence of brokered negotiations among stakeholders in a quasi-political process. PJM has followed this pattern and has implemented FERC's principles more successfully than any other ISO. At the same time, as FERC itself has conceded, Order No. 888 was itself simply a first step and not enough to fully achieve competitive markets and open access transmission. FERC perceived continuing impediments to competition, including:

- insufficient separation between generation and merchant functions
- multiple pancaked transmission rates within a region
- congestion management and loop flow problems
- generation market power that results when market size is limited by transmission constraints

In the years following Order No. 888, industry restructuring imposed new stresses on the transmission grid, including:

- divestiture by integrated utilities of more than 50,000 MW of generating capacity
- increased merger activity
- significant growth in the volume of electric power trading
- increased use of market-based rate authority
- the emergence of retail competition at the state level

Although the nation's transmission traffic increased, very little was done to increase the load serving and transfer capability of the bulk transmission system. FERC noted both economic and engineering inefficiencies:

- difficulty in determining available transmission capacity
- parallel path flows
- use of non-market approaches to managing transmission congestion
- pancaking of transmission access charges
- absence of clear transmission rights
- absence of secondary markets in transmission service
- disincentives created by the level and structure of transmission rates[21]

Regional transmission organizations

To address these and other related concerns, FERC focused on capturing maximum regional efficiency from the transmission grid through development of independent regional transmission organizations (RTOs) that may be ISOs, transcos, grid companies, or a hybrid combination. Invoking its authority under Section 202(a) of the Federal Power Act to divide the country into regional districts for the voluntary interconnection and coordination of generation and transmission facilities, FERC built on Order No. 888's initial effort to reform and restructure power pools by use of ISOs.

FERC's RTO initiative deals with several critical issues:

Independence remains a bedrock principle. RTOs must structurally separate the merchant and transmission functions of vertically integrated utilities. Experience with ISOs reinforces the importance of governance standards in achieving independence. To realize its objective of light-handed regulation, FERC requires a structural fix rather than labor-intensive behavioral mitigation.

Size matters. A system operator must have broad geographic reach to internalize loop flow, re-dispatch constrained interfaces, eliminate pancaked rates, and improve system reliability. Single-state grid organizations, such as those in New York and California, may be insufficiently competitive. FERC therefore envisages RTOs with at least the size of current regional reliability councils.

Authority. RTOs must have day-to-day and hour-to-hour authority to operate the grid, *i.e.*, the RTO must be a control area operator in order to determine transmission maintenance schedules, relieve constraints through re-dispatch, acquire and dispatch ancillary services, and calculate available transmission capacity.

Reliability. RTOs must have exclusive authority for maintaining short-term reliability of the transmission grid under its control.

Order No. 2000

FERC's Final Rule on Regional Transmission Organizations, Order No. 2000, issued in December 1999, took the next ambitious step to open wholesale electricity markets to competition. "Our objective," stated FERC, " is for all transmission-owning entities in the Nation, including non-public utilities, to place their transmission facilities under the control of RTOs in a timely manner. . . . [W]e expect jurisdictional utilities to form RTOs."[22] Although nominally voluntary, Order No. 2000 requires public utilities to make appropriate filings with FERC to initiate operation of RTOs—existing ISOs must also file.

FERC perceives an array of pro-competitive benefits from RTOs, including more efficient regional transmission pricing, improved congestion management, elimination of rate pancaking, more efficient transmission and generation planning, and reduced transaction costs. Most important, by separating control of transmission from power market participants, RTOs are thought to reduce opportunities for discrimination and market power abuse, while resulting in consumer savings over a 15-year period in excess of $5 billion per year.

Building on Order No. 888 and intervening experience, Order No. 2000 confirms four minimum characteristics of an RTO:

- independence from market participants
- regional scope
- possession of operational authority
- exclusive authority to maintain short-term reliability

Order No. 2000 also specifies eight minimum functions of an RTO, including:

- tariff administration and design
- congestion management
- parallel path flow
- ancillary services
- determination of total transmission capability available transmission capability
- market monitoring
- planning and expansion
- interregional coordination

Having provided the requisite blueprint, Order No. 2000 requires all utilities that own, operate, or control interstate transmission facilities to put them under the control of an RTO according to the following schedule:

- The RTO must be functioning by December 15, 2001
- A congestion management function must be operational by December 15, 2002
- Interregional parallel path flow coordination, transmission planning, and expansion functions must be implemented by December 15, 2004
- Termination of passive ownership must occur no later than December 15, 2006

The Final Rule contemplates either an ISO or a transco model. Any utility electing to form a transco must relinquish active ownership in transmission assets within five years of RTO approval, with the result that all transmission owners will be obliged to cede control of their transmission assets to an ISO or to a transco, having only passive ownership not later than December 15, 2006.

Because the Final Rule avoids prescribing forms of organization for RTOs or mandating that transmission owners participate in an RTO, FERC was spared deciding the extent of its statutory authority in these respects.

Under Sections 205 and 206 of the Federal Power Act, however, FERC is empowered to ensure that the rates, charges, classifications, and services of public utilities are just and reasonable and not unduly discriminatory. FERC also "has responsibility to consider . . . the anticompetitive effects of regulated aspects of interstate utility operations pursuant to Section 202 and 203, and under like directives contained in Sections 205, 206 and 207 [of the Federal Power Act]."[23] It seems clear enough that in the event of a legal test, FERC's exercise of prescriptive authority would be sustained.

In Order No. 2000 FERC chose not to exercise this authority by requiring participation in RTOs as a remedy for undue discrimination by public utilities or as a necessary condition to their receiving or retaining market-based rate authority. Similarly, Order No. 2000 avoids construing the implications of Section 202(a), which authorizes FERC "to divide the country into regional districts for the voluntary interconnection and coordination" of transmission and generation facilities. (Order No. 2000 nonetheless recites FERC's authority under Section 203 of the Federal Power Act to approve disposition of jurisdictional transmission assets by public utilities, including transfer of control of such assets to RTOs).[24] Despite the Final Rule's nominally voluntary nature, FERC's self-pronounced obligation to promote RTO operation at the earliest feasible date is unlikely to be disregarded by jurisdictional utilities.

PJM's Compliance Filing under Order No. 2000 and FERC's Response

In October 2000, PJM and its transmission owners made a joint compliance filing at FERC pursuant to Order No. 2000[25]. PJM submitted that it had satisfied all of the required characteristics and functions of an RTO. By order issued on July 12, 2001, FERC provisionally granted PJM RTO status[26]. In doing so, FERC largely agreed with PJM's submission and noted:

- PJM has operational authority over all the facilities under its control
- PJM's existing operations meet the criteria for maintaining short-term reliability

- PJM is the sole administrator and transmission provider, provides ancillary services, and is the sole OASIS administrator

FERC also noted its preference for development of very large RTOs—one for the Northeast, one for the Midwest, one for the Southeast, and one for the West. Successful large-scale RTOs would, in FERC's view, improve grid reliability, remove remaining opportunities for discriminatory transmission practices, improve market performance, and facilitate lighter-handed regulation. Significantly, FERC determined that PJM's RTO proposal should serve as a platform for a prospective unified Northeast RTO that would embody both the New England and New York ISOs, whose Order No. 2000 compliance filings were contemporaneously denied.

"We conclude," FERC stated, "that PJM's tariffs, agreements, and other governing contracts provide a sound framework that will enable PJM to expand geographically and merge with other markets in the Northeast region and to the West." To implement that conclusion and encourage a joint proposal, FERC directed PJM and the other ISOs to participate in settlement discussions at FERC.

PJM has therefore become the RTO template of choice, with profound influence over the architecture, technology, and politics of electricity restructuring in the United States. This book seeks to tell the story of PJM's transformation from an administrative adjunct to the PJM power pool to an independent, self-funded, information-based, and FERC-sanctioned regional enterprise.

Notes

[1] Joskow and Schmalensee, *Markets for Power*, 1983, pp. 104-05

[2] Henney et al., "Energy Marketing: Is There Added Value in Value Added?" 17 *Public Utilities Fortnightly* 30, 1997, pp. 16-17

[3] Barker, Tennenbaum, and Woolf, *Governance and Regulation of Power Pools and System Operators*, World Bank Technical Paper No. 382 -1997, p. 9

[4] Within a control area, generation is controlled to match the area's load plus exports and less imports. A control area has an electrical and geographical boundary. It may consist of a single utility or many utilities bound together pursuant to contractual arrangements. Technically, however, all generating utilities within a control area operate and control their combined resources to meet their combined loads as one system. Each control area has one dispatch center that monitors generation output, system frequency, and line power flows within its control area and between its control area and adjacent control areas. Each control area:

- provides enough capacity to carry its own expected load with provision for adequate reserve and regulating margin

- operates so as not to affect interchanges of energy through frequency changes or overload of another control area's transmission facilities

- continuously balances its generation against its load so that its net tie line loading agrees with its scheduled net interchange

Federal Energy Regulatory Commission, *Power Pooling in the United States*, (FERC-0049) (hereafter *Power Pooling*) (1981), pp. 26-27

[5] See prepared remarks of Robert H. Lamb, Washington representative for PJM Interconnection, L.L.C., *Hearing on Pending Electricity Legislation, United States Senate, Committee on Energy and Natural Resources*, April 11, 2000

[6] See, *e.g., Public Serv. Co. of Col.*, 58 FERC ¶ 61,322 at 62,038, 1992; Kelliher, "Pushing the Envelope: Development of Federal Electric Transmission Policy," 42 *American Univ. L. Rev.*, 1993, pp. 543, 548

[7] See *Otter Tail Power Co. v. United States*, 410 US 366, 368 (1973)

[8] 16 U.S.C. § 824b (1988)

[9] 16 U.S.C. §§ 824c-d (1988)

[10] 45 FERC ¶ 61,095 at 61,269 (1988)

[11] See *Public Serv. Co. of Col.*, 58 FERC ¶ 61,322 at 62,039 (1992)

[12] See *Florida Municipal Power Agency v. Florida Power & Light Company*, 65 FERC ¶ 61,125 (1993)

[13] See, *e.g., Hermiston Generating Company,* 69 FERC ¶ 61,025 (1994)

[14] *Promoting Wholesale Competition Through Open-access Non-discriminatory Transmission services by Public Utilities,* Final Rule, Order No. 888 [FERC Stats. & Regs., Regs. Preambles 1991-1996] ¶ 31,036 at 31,634 (1996)(hereafter *Order No. 888) Order on reh'g,* Order No. 888-A [Regs. Preambles] III FERC Stats. & Regs. ¶ 31,048 at 30,226 (1997)

[15] See, *e.g., Kansas City Power & Light,* 67 FERC ¶ 61,183 (1994)

[16] Marlette, 37 *Nat Resources J.,* 125, 130 (1997)

[17] See *Power Pooling in the United States* (FERC-0049)(1981), pp.15-23, 26-27

[18] The difference between a generator's capacity to produce electricity and its actual output is the "spinning reserve" of the unit. Spinning reserve is needed on a system to regulate, second by second, the generation output to match the load and to provide rapid replacement of power when other facilities experience outages

[19] *Order No. 888* [citation]; Mimeo, p. 268

[20] Id.

[21] *Regional Transmission organizations,* Final Rule, Order No. 2000 [Regs. Preambles], III FERC Stats.& Regs., ¶ 31,089 at 31,014 (1999)(hereafter *Order No. 2000), Order on reh'g.,* Order No. 2000-A, FERC Stats. & Regs., ¶ 31,092 (2000)

[22] *Order No. 2000,* at p. 30,933.

[23] *Order No. 2000* at p. 31,043; *Gulf States Utilities Co. v. FPC,* 411 U.S. 747, 758-59 (1973)

[24] *Order No. 2000* at p. 31,045; *El Paso Electric Company and South West Services,* 68 FERC Para. 61,181 at 61,914-15 (1994)

[25] Regional Transmission Organization, 65 FR 809 (Jan. 6, 2000), FERC Stats. & Regs. ¶ 31,089 (1999), *order on reh'g,* Order No. 2000-A, 65 FR 12,088 (March 8, 2000), FERC Stats. & Regs. ¶ 31,0992 (2000), *petitions for review pending sub nom.,* Public Utility District No. 1 of Snohomish County, Washington, v, FERC, Nos. 00-1174, *et al.* (D.C. Cir.).

[26] *PJM Interconnection, L.L.C., et al,* 96 FERC ¶ 61,061.

CHAPTER TWO

PJM's Evolution and Development

Order No. 2000 confirms that electricity is a network industry. Efficient transmission embraces more than electric throughput. It is instead a complex service with substantial network interactions, driven by efficient market design.[1] Order No. 2000 articulates that design as a blueprint for restructuring an entire industry. Accordingly, it focuses on optimum development of the network itself rather than profitability or welfare of individual transmission providers. In this context, ISOs have emerged as primary network facilitators by enhancing access, promoting short-term spot markets, defining a workable system of transmission rights, pricing transmission according to marginal costs, providing a viable means of congestion management, and balancing aggregate production and consumption continuously within the limits of the transmission system.

PJM leads this new technology and is the baseline model against which all ISOs and, ultimately RTOs, will be measured. Before achieving ISO status in 1997, PJM was a free-flowing interconnection of eight utility systems that acted as a unit to meet emergencies, increase reliability for delivering electricity, and reduce overall costs. For a timeline of events related to PJM's history see Figure 2–1. As a power pool in the pre-ISO era, PJM conferred significant economic and operational benefits on its members, including reduced installed capacity requirements, centralized unit commitment, coordinated bilateral transactions and instantaneous real-time dispatch of energy resources to meet customer load requirements. PJM was and is the largest single control area and tight power pool in North America.

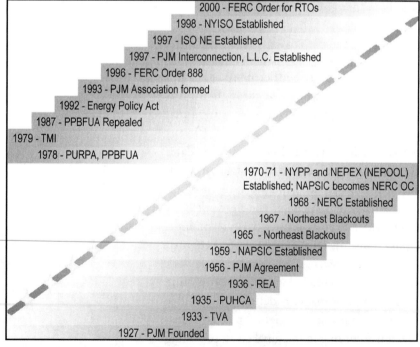

2000 - FERC Order for RTOs
1998 - NYISO Established
1997 - ISO NE Established
1997 - PJM Interconnection, L.L.C. Established
1996 - FERC Order 888
1993 - PJM Association formed
1992 - Energy Policy Act
1987 - PPBFUA Repealed
1979 - TMI
1978 - PURPA, PPBFUA
1970-71 - NYPP and NEPEX (NEPOOL) Established; NAPSIC becomes NERC OC
1968 - NERC Established
1967 - Northeast Blackouts
1965 - Northeast Blackouts
1959 - NAPSIC Established
1956 - PJM Agreement
1936 - REA
1935 - PUHCA
1933 - TVA
1927 - PJM Founded

Fig. 2-1 PJM's History and the History of the Electric Industry Regulation

PA-NJ Agreement

PJM's existence as a tight power pool dates from 1927, when PSE&G, PECO and PP&L—three of its constituent utilities—became signatories to the first power pool agreement, the PA-NJ Agreement. The PA-NJ pool continued for almost 30 years until expanded to its present configuration as PJM in 1956. For several years prior to 1927 the utilities had already realized pooling benefits through interconnection of separate stations on their respective systems, including reductions in installed and capacity reserves, lower operating costs, and improved service reliability. In addition, during the 1920s interconnections had already been established between PECO, PP&L, Atlantic Electric, Delmarva Power, Pepco, BG&E, and the several GPU utilities.

An economic justification study showed gross annual savings of almost $50 million, principally attributable to seasonal-load and reserve diversity. Equally important, however, utilities were responding then as now to a government initiative—the Hoover Superpower Conference of 1923, convened by Secretary of Commerce Hoover to consider cooperative federal-state promotion of superpower development in the Eastern Seaboard Zone. The Commission recommended extension of interconnections between systems, an early form of regionalization.

Under the PA-NJ Agreement each utility was responsible for financing, controlling, and connecting with a segment of a newly constructed 235-mile 220 kV transmission ring, linking various power stations and terminals within Pennsylvania and New Jersey, completed in 1932. The PA-NJ Agreement also required each utility to make internal transmission available for power interchange (subject to separate metering), share load and reserve diversity, and render mutual assistance in emergencies.

Each utility designated a representative to serve on a three-member operating committee that functioned by unanimous consent. A load scheduling and operating group, formed as a permanent committee with representatives of all member companies, determined diversity entitlements and obligations. Eventually it also acquired responsibility for coordinating the maintenance of all major generating units in the pool, load forecasting, and installed capacity deficiency accounting.

PJM Agreement of 1956

In 1955 BG&E and GPU (including its four operating subsidiaries)[2] joined PSE&G, PECO, and PP&L as members of the PA-NJ operating committee. On September 26, 1956 the parties entered into the PJM Agreement, which (subject to numerous updating amendments)[3] became the principal organic document of the PJM power pool until its restructuring as an ISO in 1997.

The PJM Agreement provided for a Management Committee and an operating committee as successors to the operating committee and operating group under the prior agreement. The Management Committee in turn established a Maintenance Committee and a Planning and Engineering Committee. It also created an Office of the Interconnection (OI) to conduct all pool operations, although all regular personnel of the OI were initially PECO employees and functioned within PECO's system operations division. In 1970 the OI was relocated to a new control center in Valley Forge, Pennsylvania. PECO nonetheless remained responsible for all of PJM's administrative functions and business activities until 1993.

The PJM Agreement addressed several critical pool-related issues.

Installed capacity requirements and obligations

A power pool permits participating utilities to reduce the amount of installed capacity required in a coordinated system as compared to the aggregate of individual utility requirements in the absence of pooling. Optimum benefits result when the installed capacity requirement accommodates load diversity, seasonal load shape, deviations of load about the mean, planned maintenance of generating capacity, and diversity in forced outages of generating capacity. To achieve those benefits the pool must equitably determine each participant's respective obligation and have in place an appropriate accounting formula allowing it to equalize installed capacity deficiencies and excesses on a forward-looking basis.

Under the PJM Agreement, the electric generating capacity of the pool is "the amount of capacity sufficient to carry the load, permit maintenance and provide reserve adequate to achieve a high degree of reliability." The management committee determines the forecast requirement for such capacity for specified planning periods and allocates each member utility's "equitable share" pursuant to a formula.[4] The formula accords recognition to factors that materially affect the installed capacity requirement, including a forced outage rate adjustment, an adjustment for the effect of large units above a specified size, and a load drop adjustment that recognizes the impact of different system load shapes.

To provide the basis for the management committee's determination, each member utility is required to submit its plans for carrying its share by:

- installation of generating capacity
- purchases of generating capacity independent of the PJM Agreement, either from member utilities or others
- purchases of additional required generating capacity from other member utilities having excess at specified rates pursuant to the PJM Agreement

Each member utility's plans constitute a firm commitment as of a date two years before the beginning of each planning period, at which time each must plan to install or arrange for sufficient capacity and related transmission facilities to carry its equitable share of the forecast requirement, *i.e.*, to supply, if needed, the energy requirements of its own load and its allocated share of spinning reserve and regulating capacity. June 1 of a year through May 31 of the following year is used as the planning period since the PJM pool as a whole has a summer peak. Purchased capacity is intended to meet incidental deficiencies and unpredictable changes in load, not a party's underlying obligation.

Accounting for capacity deficiency transactions for a planning period takes place only during that period. Adjustments are made, if necessary, to previously projected transactions to harmonize differences between actual and forecast capacity conditions, both as to a member utility and the PJM system as a whole. In addition, forecast obligations are adjusted to reflect differences between experienced and forecast average load and unavailable capability during the planning period. All deficiency transactions are charged and paid for at a specified rate, intended to promote coordination of capacity installations by furnishing the prospective buyer with reasonable short-term alternatives and the supplier with a fair return on investment.[5]

Operating capacity requirement and obligations

Day-to-day operation of a power pool was managed to:

- meet load requirements economically
- provide protection against the hazards of load deviation from forecast levels
- provide frequency regulation
- regulate power flow on interconnection ties

To do this, the PJM Agreement established an operating capacity requirement, *i.e.,* "the amount of capacity in operation, or capable of operation within a specified time, sufficient to carry the load on any day and to provide [an adequate] reserve . . ."[6] The PJM Agreement also established a daily operating reserve requirement, taking into account the probability of load deviations from forecast, equipment malfunction or failure, load level, time of day, and season of the year. A portion of the operating reserve requirement was synchronized to provide spinning reserve (spinning reserve requirement). A proportional share of the spinning reserve requirement was then allocated to each member utility based on the ratio of its average load at the time of the system peak load each week to the average system peak loads each week[7](Fig. 2-2).

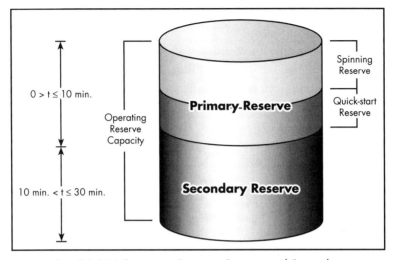

Fig. 2-2 PJM Operating Review—Primary and Secondary

Determination of the operating reserve requirement—first by the individual utilities that came to comprise PJM and then as a pool requirement—can be traced from an early ad hoc approach to eventual use of sophisticated probability techniques. Initially the spinning reserve capacity of an individual utility was equal to that of the largest unit on its system, often as much as 25% of its peak load. In a pooling operation, however, the most significant hazard was deviation of load from the daily forecast by an amount exceeding the pool's largest unit. For an extended period before 1956, load forecasting deviation probability curves were based on the pool's historic daytime and evening peak periods. In 1956, when PJM's peak load was just under 8,000 MW, minimum spinning reserves equaled 385 MW for daytime peaks and 347 MW for evening peaks, *i.e.*, 5% and 4-1/2%, respectively.

Eventually PJM developed a computer program to determine the operating reserve requirement, divided into spinning reserve and scheduled reserve. Spinning reserve equaled the capacity of the largest unit operating within the pool plus an allowance for regulating capacity, was synchronized to the grid, and could be loaded in 10 minutes or less. Scheduled reserve could be loaded to scheduled capacity in 30 minutes or less. The computer program addressed the probability of two hazards—load forecasting and forced outages of generating capacity. It indicated the probability of just carrying or failing to carry the load for various amounts of scheduled operating reserve at different load levels and load forecasting deviations.

PJM later adopted a more sophisticated definition of operating reserve. In place of spinning reserve and scheduled reserve, the new definition divided operating reserve into:

- *Primary reserve, i.e.,* operating capability synchronized to the grid or on standby and capable of being loaded within 10 minutes or less, subdivided into *spinning reserve* (that portion of primary reserve synchronized to the grid and under unrestricted control of the turbine-generator) and *quick-start reserve* (any remaining portion of primary reserve that need not be synchronized to the grid but capable of being loaded as needed)
- *Secondary reserve, i.e.,* operating capability that is either synchronized to the grid or on standby and capable of being loaded within 30 minutes

Eventually PJM developed an advanced computer program to measure risks in real time, particularly outage probability, and determine reserve objectives for given levels of risk. Primary reserve was then determined based on the probability of forced outages only, and secondary reserve was equal to the largest generator's output but not less than 700 MW. Allocation of operating reserve to the member utilities was based on statistical peak load, adjusted on a seasonal basis.[8]

PJM's organization

Under the PJM Agreement each member utility appointed one representative to the Management Committee, which initially had five members but eventually expanded to eight when PEPCO, Atlantic Electric, and Delmarva Power joined PJM in subsequent years.

Certain actions of the Management Committee required unanimous assent, including amendment of the PJM Agreement itself, a change in the percentage applied to the forecast planning period system peak to determine the forecast reserve requirement for any planning period, and a change that would increase any member utility's capital investment or operating expenses by more than a stipulated percentage of its electric operating revenue for the preceding calendar year.[9] Action on other matters was determined by weighted voting, based on each member utility's peak load during three immediately preceding planning periods and requiring combined weighted votes of at least 75% of the total.

The PJM Agreement also established the OI and placed it under direction of a Manager with specific duties and responsibilities that are precursors of certain functions ultimately assumed by PJM as an ISO, including:

- coordination of the operation and maintenance of the system's bulk power supply facilities, used for load and reactive supply, "to maintain reliability of service and obtain . . . maximum overall economies"
- coordination of the system's bulk power supplies with other systems "to secure reliability and continuity of services and other advantages of pooling on a *regional* basis" (emphasis added)
- coordination of interchange accounting
- consultation with the operating committee and the planning and engineering committee (the members of which are appointed by the management committee)
- preparation of operating studies of the system's bulk power supply facilities, leading to recommendation and actions "necessary to maintain reliable operation . . ."

By 1973 PJM was technologically and organizationally capable of centrally dispatching generation within the pool through the OI. It therefore adopted a policy formally recognizing the pool as a single system under economic dispatch within the constraints of reliability and fuel availability.

The PJM Agreement also provided that each member of the management committee appoint representatives to serve on the operating committee and the planning and engineering committee.

The operating committee's charge involved establishment and revision of operating principles, practices and procedures, with particular reference to reliability of the system's power supply facilities, including location, character, and amounts of spinning reserve and regulating capacity, adequacy of automatic control, sources and need for reactive capacity, voltage schedules, and other pertinent conditions.

The planning and engineering committee addressed the overall design and reliability of the system's bulk power supply facilities and planning for generating capacity, reactive capability and voltage control, and transmission facilities. Other duties included recommendation to the management committee of a forecast requirement for electric generating capacity, allocation of the forecast requirement to each member utility, and maintenance of a continuing composite long-range plan to provide adequate and reliable service.

Coordinated operation

The PJM Agreement reflected the tension between each member utility's right to control its own facilities and services and the pool's need for coordinated planning and operation. The PJM Agreement confirmed that each member utility would retain sole control over its wholly owned facilities, which would always be first available to the owner for its own use. In the transition to ISO status, as noted above, these principles were superseded.

At the same time the PJM Agreement required each member utility to provide for sufficient transmission connecting its own generating plants to the grid for delivery of its equitable share of the forecast requirement as adjusted. To achieve this objective each member utility was required to:

- deliver to its customers the output of its own electric generating plants without relying on the transmission facilities of any other member utility, except those with which contractual arrangements have been made
- include in any contractual arrangements for the sale or purchase of bulk power, whether from a member utility or a third party, adequate provisions to meet its transmission obligations

- provide sufficient reactive capability and voltage control facilities to (i) meet the reactive requirements of the system and (ii) adequately maintain voltage levels required by the system's bulk power supply facilities
- coordinate the operating schedules of its generating facilities with those of other member utilities maintaining reliable service and obtaining maximum operating economies
- coordinate its schedules of planned outages of generation and transmission facilities with those of other member utilities in order to maintain reliable and economic operation of the system
- coordinate with other member utilities and third parties in the planning and operation of the *regional* bulk power supply facilities to secure a high level of reliability and continuity of service and other advantages of pooling on a *regional* basis
- adopt pool-wide standards for system design, equipment ratings, operating practices, and maintenance practices
- cooperate in implementing uniform and pool-wide emergency procedures
- maintain a proportion of its load subject to control by automatic under-frequency load-shedding devices approved by the management committee

Planning and reliability

The foregoing operational requirements applied in the context of an ongoing exercise, conducted by the planning and engineering committee, to review, evaluate, and coordinate planning for the pool's generating capacity, reactive capability and voltage control, and transmission facilities. Each member utility was required to submit its individual plans to the committee for the addition, modification, and removal of generation and bulk power transmission facilities. From these plans the committee was charged with developing a continuing composite long-range plan to provide adequate and reliable service in accordance with planning principles established by the management committee.

Under the PJM Agreement the planning principles were to be consistent with those of the Mid-Atlantic Area Council (MAAC), organized in 1967 as a consequence of the northeast power system blackout of 1965.[10] MAAC was launched "[t]o augment . . . the reliability of the bulk electric supply systems of the signatories through a higher degree of coordination planning of their generation and transmission facilities."[11] MAAC promulgates principles and standards for planning bulk electric supply systems and enters into inter-area coordination agreements with other NERC regions (Fig. 2-3). MAAC's policy was consistent with PJM's contemporaneous adoption of two broad reliability principles, reflected in the PJM Agreement:

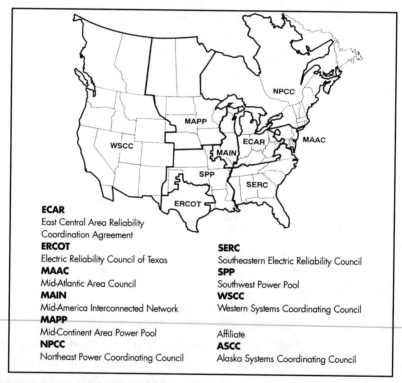

ECAR
East Central Area Reliability
Coordination Agreement
ERCOT
Electric Reliability Council of Texas
MAAC
Mid-Atlantic Area Council
MAIN
Mid-America Interconnected Network
MAPP
Mid-Continent Area Power Pool
NPCC
Northeast Power Coordinating Council

SERC
Southeastern Electric Reliability Council
SPP
Southwest Power Pool
WSCC
Western Systems Coordinating Council

Affiliate
ASCC
Alaska Systems Coordinating Council

Fig. 2-3 NERC Regions, Including MAAC

- Each PJM member utility was to plan its own generation and bulk power transmission system within the framework of PJM's long-range plans and policies
- The planning and engineering committee was to review and coordinate individual plans to assure collectively that they provide the desired reliability for the PJM interconnection

In planning exercises of this kind, a reliable bulk power system presupposes a sufficient margin of generating capability over expected load, and sufficient transmission paths between generation and load, so the probability of continued service is at least equal to some agreed reliability standard. The loads, generation capabilities, and transmission capabilities of all the system's participants affect the satisfactory performance of an interconnected system. The most economical balance between generation and transmission reliability therefore requires careful consideration. There is always a tradeoff between adding generating reserve capacity and installing additional transmission facilities to achieve an equivalent reliability benefit, although transmission only provides access to reserve capacity and cannot substitute for it.

Under the PJM Agreement, once the committee determined that an individual member utility's plan could adversely affect overall regional reliability, it was empowered to modify the relevant operating practices and procedures to provide for an adequate level of operating reserve (including consideration of location, character and amounts of spinning reserve and regulation capacity, adequacy of automatic control, sources and need for reactive capacity, voltage schedules, and maintenance outages, load shedding, etc.). In this way autonomous operations of PJM's member utilities were subordinated to system-wide planning imperatives.

EHV Agreement

In 1967 the PJM member utilities entered into the Extra High Voltage Transmission System Agreement (EHV Agreement), which was supplemented several times during the next decades. The EHV Agreement allocated rights and obligations among PJM's member utilities with respect to a 500 kV transmission system (the EHV system). Initially, the EHV system transmitted power from the Keystone and Conemaugh mine mouth power plants in which the member utilities owned undivided percentage interests. The power generated was to be used by member utilities in accordance with those interests and for the interchange of capacity and energy with third parties. The EHV Agreement was later supplemented to include transmission of power from the Peach Bottom, Salem, and Three Mile Island nuclear plants. Eventually the EHV system totaled more than 1,500 miles.

Although each member utility assumed responsibility for constructing, operating and maintaining its respective portion of the EHV system, coordination of switching, voltage levels and scheduling of maintenance remained subject to the PJM Agreement. Monthly charges and credits were determined in accordance with each party's percentage participation in and use of the EHV system. A representative administrative committee, appointed under the EHV Agreement, provided managerial oversight.

PJM Interconnection Association

The PJM Agreement contemplated a jointly supported office of the interconnection to manage the PJM system, and from 1970 that office was housed in a separate control center in Valley Forge, Pennsylvania. Prior to July 1993, however, the business activities of the pool were managed by PECO Energy Systems, a member utility, whose load dispatchers also served in that capacity for the office of the interconnection. In 1993 all administrative functions of the pool became the responsibility of PJM Interconnection Association (PJMIA), an unincorporated association jointly managed on behalf of PJM's utility members. PJMIA maintained its own staff, had operating rights and obligations, but did not maintain an ownership interest in office real estate, operating equipment, or the transmission system itself.

Nonetheless PJMIA served as the nucleus around which the PJM ISO was ultimately built. Through 1996 PJMIA operated a free-flowing interconnection of eight electric utility systems, acting as a unit to meet emergencies, increasing reliability for delivering electricity, and reducing costs to the system as a whole. Member systems continued to receive revenues and pay charges under the terms of the PJM Agreement for internal and external energy-related transactions. The Management Committee, as established by the PJM Agreement and representing each member utility, set policies for governance of the pool. Although PJMIA was responsible for carrying out those policies and lacked autonomy, it eventually became the focus of change in response to Order No. 888's concern that "utilities can continue to trade with a selective group within a power pool that discriminatorily excludes others from becoming a member and that provides preferential intra-pool transmission rights and rates."[12]

Notes

[1] See, *e.g.,* William W. Hogan, FERC Policy on Regional Transmission Organizations: Comments in Response to the Notice of Proposed Rulemaking, FERC Docket No. RM99-2-000, August 16, 1999

[2] The GPU operating companies include Pennsylvania Electric Company, Metropolitan Edison Company, New Jersey Power & Light Company, and Jersey Central Power & Light Company

[3] Supplemental agreements were entered into on January 28, 1965; November 19, 1970; April 1, 1974; June 15, 1977; and March 26, 1981 to reflect such amendments

[4] PJM Agreement, Schedule 2.21, Revision No. 1

[5] PJM Agreement, Schedule 4.01, Revision No. 13

[6] PJM Agreement, § 7.1

[7] PJM Agreement, Schedule 6.02

[8] PJM Agreement, Schedule 6.02

[9] PJM Agreement, § 3.2(c)

[10] The blackout led to major changes to improve reliability. Although cascading transmission trippings caused major load interruptions only in portions of Ontario, New York state and New England, the industry reviewed all systems to mitigate the impact of power system disturbances. MAAC was organized shortly after the blackout

[11] PJM Agreement, Appendix D

[12] Order No. 888, Mimeo, p. 268

CHAPTER THREE

PJM's Transition to ISO Status

In 1996, as FERC prepared to issue Order No. 888, the PJM utilities were engaged in framing a massive restructuring plan intended to transform PJMIA into an ISO that would administer both a pool-wide open access transmission tariff and a competitive regional wholesale electricity market.[1] Development of the plan proved to be contentious. PECO Energy broke from the other PJM member utilities, largely due to the majority's preferred method of transmission pricing and congestion management. When PJM filed the restructuring plan at FERC in July 1996, PECO Energy declined to support it and shortly thereafter filed a competing plan.

To implement its restructuring, PJM relied on several platform agreements:

- Transmission Owners Agreement (to which the PJM control area open access transmission tariff was a schedule)
- Mid-Atlantic Market Operations Agreement
- Reserve Sharing Agreement
- PJM Independent System Operator Agreement
- PJM Dispute Resolution Agreement

Transmission Owners Agreement

The Transmission Owners Agreement (TOA) addressed two critical functions: establishment of an open access transmission tariff for the PJM control area (PJM tariff) and vesting in an ISO responsibility for administering the tariff and managing the bulk power transmission facilities in the PJM control area. The TOA contemplated that the transmission owners would enter into a services agreement with an ISO (the ISO Agreement or ISOA) pursuant to which the ISO would:

- operate the PJM control area
- direct and coordinate operation of designated transmission facilities in the PJM control area (*i.e.*, facilities with nominal voltage of 230 kV or higher together with other key transmission facilities)
- administer the PJM tariff, including determination of available transmission capacity and the filing of PJM tariff changes "on behalf of" the transmission owners"[2]
- administer a protocol for the regional transmission expansion planning of bulk power transmission facilities, including development of a regional transmission expansion plan
- coordinate planned outages of designated transmission facilities
- develop guidelines for operation of transmission facilities in the PJM control area
- perform studies on the reliability, availability, and capacity on bulk power transmission facilities in the PJM control area
- operate the PJM open access same-time information system (OASIS)[3] (Fig. 3-1)

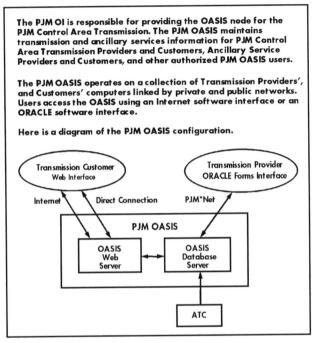

The PJM OI is responsible for providing the OASIS node for the PJM Control Area Transmission. The PJM OASIS maintains transmission and ancillary services information for PJM Control Area Transmission Providers and Customers, Ancillary Service Providers and Customers, and other authorized PJM OASIS users.

The PJM OASIS operates on a collection of Transmission Providers', and Customers' computers linked by private and public networks. Users access the OASIS using an Internet software interface or an ORACLE software interface.

Here is a diagram of the PJM OASIS configuration.

Fig. 3–1 The PJM OASIS

Although initially confined to PJM member utilities, the TOA contemplated, as additional parties, entities owning bulk power transmission facilities capable of being integrated into the PJM control area, and being operated on the basis of free flowing ties with existing transmission facilities.[4] All parties to the TOA were obligated "to provide the ISO with the financial support, information, and other resources necessary to carry out the functions described earlier."[5] The obligation would include funding the acquisition of land, structures, fixtures, equipment and facilities, and other capital expenditures for the ISO. ISO costs were to be allocated on an equal *per capita* basis to each TOA party up to 10% of total costs; remaining costs were to be allocated on a weighted basis.

The TOA required each party to provide service over its transmission facility in accordance with the PJM tariff integrating the delivery of electric capacity and energy from resources to loads served by the party receiving such service. The TOA prescribed zonal rates for transmission service in accordance with the PJM tariff. Zonal rates for network services were to be based on the revenue requirements of the transmission owner or owners in the zone within which the customer's network load is located, subject to a 10% distance differential for deliveries outside that zone.

The TOA established an administrative committee. Each party was entitled to appoint a member to represent its interests. The administrative committee was empowered to approve and, if necessary, adjust the ISO's capital budget and the transmission owners' portion of its operating budget. By two-thirds vote the administrative committee could also terminate or amend the ISO Agreement. In addition, the TOA could nominate two "affiliated directors" to serve on the board of directors of the ISO, retain the power to remove the ISO, select a new ISO, approve a new service agreement with a new ISO, or assign the ISO Agreement. As will be noted, the transmission owners' effort to retain a substantial measure of control over the ISO was deemed to contravene the cardinal principle of ISO independence and drew FERC's objection accordingly.

PJM Tariff

The proposed PJM tariff was filed after FERC's promulgation of a *pro forma* tariff in Order No. 888 and thus incorporated most of its provisions (Fig 3-2). There were nonetheless certain significant differences.

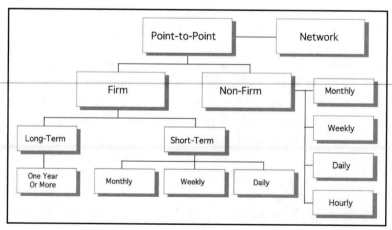

Fig. 3–2 PJM Transmission Services Offered in the Control Area

Unlike the *pro forma* tariff, the PJM tariff required zonal pricing for network service. Under the zonal pricing proposal, the PJM utilities divided the PJM control area into 10 zones corresponding to their existing service territories. Because of the reciprocal nature of network service, the network customer was granted the right to deliver energy and capacity to its network load from network resources anywhere within the PJM control area or delivered to the PJM control area from external sources or from the bulk power market. Transmission customers were required to pay for network transmission service based on the revenue requirement of the transmission owner or owners in whose territory its load was located, although the PJM utilities would provide each other reciprocal network and ancillary services at no charge (Table 3-1). Each PJM utility would levy a 10% surcharge for delivery of capacity and energy from resources located outside the zone in which the customer's load was located. The PJM utilities stated "inclusion of a distance differential will provide the appropriate economic signal that deliveries from more distant resources require more facilities than deliveries from a resource located more closely to the load"[6].

Application Information

A completed application must provide all of the information included in 18 CFR § 2.20 including, but not limited, to the following:

- The identity of the PJM Member requesting service
- A statement that the Member is an eligible customer under the Tariff
- A description of the Network Load at each delivery point.
- The amount and location of any interruptible loads included or to be included as an adjustment to the capacity obligation of the customer.
- A description of Network Resources (current and 10-year projection),
- Description of eligible customer's transmission system:
- Service commencement date and the term of the requested Network Transmission Service. The minimum term for the Network Transmission Service is one year.

Table 3-1 PJM Network Service Requests

The zonal pricing proposal drew criticism from intervenors, who argued for a single, grid-wide transmission rate for network transmission services. Intervenors contended that zonal pricing would violate FERC's comparability principle because similarly situated native load and network customers would pay disparate rates and transmission owners would not be required to charge themselves the same rates, *i.e.,* the proposed network rates would not apply to the PJM utilities' resources.[7]

For similar reasons the 10% surcharge also proved objectionable. Since PJM is an interconnected grid that operates as a single control area, intervenors saw no basis for a surcharge applicable to power transfers across zones. The surcharge was also thought likely to induce customers to limit their participation in the generation market to resources close to their loads, giving PJM utilities an unfair competitive advantage.

Under the PJM tariff, a point-to-point customer could wheel through or out of the PJM control area by paying a single average rate reflecting the revenue requirements of all transmission owners within the control area, but point-to-point service was not available for transactions into or within the PJM control area. Point-to-point service included firm, non-firm, long-term, or short-term service. All firm point-to-point customers were required to pay transmission congestion costs based on differences in locational prices, with firm point-to-point customers eligible for rebates of those congestion charges.[8] Non-firm point-to-point customers could elect to avoid curtailment or interruption by paying transmission congestion costs[9] (Table 3-2).

Point-to-Point Transmission Services requests are entered by market participants through the Open Access Same Time Information System (OASIS). In order to use OASIS as an eligible Transmission Service Customer, PJM requires all applicants to complete a Transmission Service Enabling Agreement. Once complete, the application must be approved by FERC. The application process is as follows:

1. Request a Transmission Service Application Form from PJM OI.
2. Complete and return application to PJM Customer Relations and Training Department.
3. If approved, PJM will forward to FERC for further approval.
4. Following approval by FERC, applicant is an eligible customer. If not approved, applicant will be notified.

All Point-to-Point Transmission Service Requests are made on OASIS and require the following information:

- Path-name
- Point of service
- Source
- Sink
- Time block
- Capacity
- Capacity type
- Begin and end date/time

Table 3–2 PJM Point-to-Point and Network Import Transmission Service Requests

Type of Request	Request Procedure
Short-Term Firm Transmission Service Requests	**PJM OASIS**
Monthly	No later than 14 days prior to the commencement of service
Weekly	No earlier than 14 days prior to the commencement of service
Daily	No earlier than three PJM business days prior to the commencement of service
Short-Term Non-Firm Transmission Service Requests	**PJM OASIS**
Monthly	No earlier than 60 days prior to the commencement of service
Weekly	No earlier than 14 days prior to the commencement of service
Daily	No earlier than two PJM business days prior to the commencement of service
Long-Term Firm Requests	**PJM OASIS and written request submitted to PJM OI containing the following information:**
	A written request for long-term transmission service submitted to the Customer Relations and Training Department
	Review of the request by the System Planning Department
	Applicant notified as to the results of the review
	Department will either approve request or begin System Impact Study process
PJM Network Import	**PJM OASIS**
Transmission Service Request	*A separate non-firm point-to-point transmission request must be made for delivery of non-designated resources to designated loads exceeding a company's load* under certain circumstances

Table 3–2 (continued)

The PJM tariff also allocated rights to the capacity benefit margin, *i.e.*, the amount of transmission interconnection capability necessary to ensure access to generation from interconnected systems not a part of the PJM control area. Initially, capacity benefit margin rights were to be allocated on a load ratio basis to parties to the Reserve Sharing Agreement, each of whom would be responsible for an allocated share of related fixed costs as either a network customer or a transmission owner providing service to its native load customers. The Reserve Sharing Agreement prohibited the non-curtailable use, sale, or transfer of rights to the capacity benefit margin. Otherwise, however, capacity benefit margin rights were assignable under the PJM tariff. The holder of such rights could deliver energy into the PJM control area on a non-firm basis and would be entitled to transmission congestion charge credits (Table 3-3).

To prevent unreliable operation due to an over-committed transmission system, it is necessary to preserve a portion of the transmission network capability in order to insure that the transmission system remains secure under a wide range of varying conditions. Margin must be preserved on the interconnected network to provide the necessary flexibility to reliably address changes in transmission capability caused by maintenance and forced outages of generation and transmission equipment, higher than expected customer loads, shared activation of reserves and changes in other operating conditions.

To ensure the integrity of the transmission system, Capacity Benefit Margin (CBM) and Transmission Reliability Margins (TRM) are applied to determine available Available Transmission Capacity (ATC). Margins are applied differently depending on the time frame and path direction of the analysis. Some margins are applied only to determine Firm ATC, since Non-Firm transactions can be curtailed. The following table provides a general description of CBM and TRM.

Margin Components

Capacity Benefit Margin	Transmission Reliability Margin
PJM applies CBM to calculate Firm ATC when P PJM is the Sink. CBM is an annual calculation based on the results of the PJM Import Capability Study (PICS). CBM is reduced in Near-Term ATC calculations when excess system reserves exist.	PJM uses 3 components of TRM depending on path direction and transmission service type. Components are: – Load Forecast Error – Unanticipated Loop Flow – Normal Operating Margin

Table 3–3 PJM Margin Components

Intervenors objected to the PJM tariff's limitation of point-to-point service to exports from the control area and transactions passing completely through the control area as "an unwarranted and unjustifiable departure from [FERC's] pro forma tariff."[10]

The PJM tariff called for ancillary services "to maintain reliability within and among the Control Areas affected by the transmission service." The ISO was to provide (or arrange for), and the transmission customer was required to purchase scheduling, system control and dispatch, and reactive supply and voltage control from generation sources—the former at a cost-based rate and the latter at a cost to be determined. The remaining ancillary services were to be provided at rates set by the Mid-Atlantic Market[11] and could be acquired by the transmission customer through the ISO, from a third party, or by self-supply. However, the transmission customer could not decline the ISO's offer of ancillary services unless it could show it had acquired services of equal quality from another deliverable source. These provisions encountered objection from intervenors as unnecessary and discriminatory, while the proposal for market-based pricing was deemed unsupported by market analysis.[12]

Rates prescribed by the PJM tariff for network customers, including the 10% differential for distant network resources, were designed to recover the revenue requirements of the transmission owners providing service in the zone in which the rates were applicable. Any additional revenues received for point-to-point service were to be credited to those entities holding firm transmission rights.[13] The rates for each zone reflected the costs of each of the constituent PJM utilities. The rates for wheeling through and wheeling out reflected the average of the zonal rates.

Mid-Atlantic Market Operations Agreement

A signal feature of PJM's filing was its inclusion under the ISO's authority of the Mid-Atlantic Market, a regional wholesale market for bulk electric energy and related services at market-based prices for qualified buyers and sellers.

Under the Mid-Atlantic Market Operations Agreement (MOA) sellers wishing to sell into the Mid-Atlantic Market would be required to submit offers setting forth prices and other operating data specified by the ISO for energy and related services on a day-ahead basis. Similarly, buyers within the PJM control area would submit load forecasts, and buyers outside the PJM control area would submit projected purchase levels and prices at which they were willing to make purchases. Market participants would also submit schedules for bilateral transactions into or out of the PJM control area and for any self-scheduled generation.

Using the information submitted, the ISO would determine the least-cost means of satisfying projected hourly energy, operating reserves, and other ancillary services requirements of the market buyers, including the reliability requirements of the PJM control area. At the same time the ISO would inform each market seller whether its offer for the following day had been accepted. Acceptance would entitle the seller to payment for its start-up and no-load costs if such costs had been separately provided and payments for energy delivered during the subsequent dispatch did not cover such costs. Within the same time frame, the ISO would then post on its OASIS[14] its forecast of the location and duration of any expected transmission congestion and of the range of differences in locational marginal prices between major sub-areas of the PJM control area expected to result from such transmission congestion.

Beginning at midnight following the noon offer deadline, the ISO would then schedule and dispatch the generation selected by it on the basis of day-ahead offers. Scheduling and dispatch of generation would reflect the prices and operating characteristics offered by market sellers using bid-based, security-constrained dispatch, and continuing until sufficient generation is dispatched in each hour to service all Mid-Atlantic Market energy purchase and ancillary service requirements. The prices for energy bought and sold in the Mid-Atlantic Market would reflect the hourly locational marginal price at each load and generation bus, as fixed by the ISO. Transmission congestion charges, determined by the differences in locational marginal prices in each hour between load and generation buses caused by transmission constraints would then be collected from all transactions causing or contributing to congestion (Fig. 3-3).

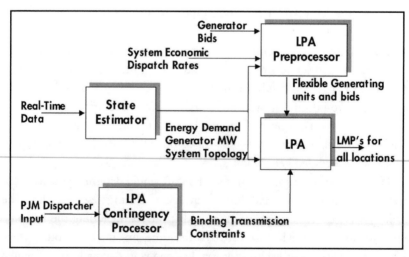

Fig 3–3 PJM Locational Pricing Model

During the dispatch day, self-scheduled generation or generation not selected for pool dispatch by the ISO would be self-scheduled. Market participants could also enter into bilateral transactions, subject to the ISO's right to recall capacity for reliability purposes.

To set overall policies for operation of the Mid-Atlantic Market, the MOA established a market administrative committee, which was also to be responsible for monitoring market performance and the ISO's market-related operating practices and regulatory filings. The ISO was nonetheless to remain responsible for day-to-day market operations. Each market participant was entitled to have a representative on the market administrative committee, with voting power weighted in accordance with each participant's volume of energy transactions during a rolling 12-month period.

Reserve Sharing Agreement

As noted, the PJM Interconnection Agreement placed great emphasis on reserve sharing and forecasting as a means of realizing economies of scale and greater reliability. The Reserve Sharing Agreement (RSA) included as parties the load-serving entities in the PJM control areas (*i.e.,* in the first instance, the transmission owners) and built explicitly on that foundation. To do so it established a contractual framework to:

- share capacity resources to reduce overall reserve requirements
- provide assistance during emergencies
- shed load if system conditions so required

The RSA sought to preserve one of the fundamental benefits of membership in the PJM power pool—a lower aggregate reserve requirement than would be obtained if each constituent utility operated on a freestanding basis. The RSA's reserve requirement calculation reflected diversities among PJM's utility members, PJM's ability to rely on a large pool of reserve resources, and import capacity drawing on emergency reserves from neighboring control areas.

Under the RSA overall reserve requirements were to be planned two years in advance. Once capacity obligations were set for a planning period, each party was required to plan, install, or contract for capacity resources to meet its individual obligation. If a party failed to satisfy its capacity obligations, it would be assessed a deficiency charge, subject to escalation discouraging repeated or significant leaning on the resources of other parties.

The parties to the RSA were also required to coordinate capacity resource plans, share capacity resources as required, provide for reactive capability and voltage control, maintain required levels of load-shedding, black start capability and operating reserves, and coordinate generator maintenance outages. The RSA imposed charges on parties that failed to comply with the instructions of the ISO in an emergency to implement active load management, reduce voltage, or drop load.

The RSA's governing body was a Reserve Sharing Committee to which each party (initially, existing PJM members but not the ISO itself) named a representative. The committee's principal responsibilities were to:

- establish the overall reserve requirement for the parties as a group and the capacity obligations of individual parties
- establish planning principles, procedures, and standards addressing the adequacy and reliability of bulk power supply
- coordinate with the ISO and administrative committees established under the TOA and MOA to establish the forecast pool requirement[15] for capacity resources[16] and criteria for use of capacity resources and serving load during emergencies

The Reserve Sharing Committee had sweeping authority over the ISO, including the power to monitor and review its performance, determine whether the ISO had failed to perform in a satisfactory fashion with respect to matters directly affecting the parties, resolve conflicts with the ISO, request modification to the services provided by the ISO and the related performance standards, and direct the ISO to make required regulatory filings.[17] In addition, the parties to the RSA by its terms *delegated* to the ISO certain responsibilities for its implementation, including establishment of the capability and deliverability of capacity resources, energy transfer in emergencies, load shedding, and the like.[18] Since the parties to the RSA were load serving entities within the PJM control area, the RSA was a transparent means of enabling the transmission owners to control the ISO, which would be independent in name but not in practice.

PJM Independent System Operator Agreement

As originally conceived by the transmission owners, PJM Services Company (Services), a Delaware not-for-profit membership corporation, was to serve as independent system operator (ISO). Services' governing body was a seven-person board of directors, two of whom were to be affiliated with members of the existing PJM pool, *i.e.*, with transmission owners. The remaining directors were not to be affiliated with any entity engaged in the generation, transmission, distribution, purchase, or sale of electric energy in the Mid-Atlantic Region.

The presence of two affiliated directors was thought to provide for "effective transfer of institutional knowledge and expertise in the operation of a complex control area."[19] In addition, affiliated directors assured "a level of protection for investments of the transmission owners who have turned over the coordination and direction of their designated transmission facilities to an independent entity."[20] The transmission owners were deemed to have a continuing fiduciary obligation to their shareholders and bondholders to maintain the value of the transferred assets. An affiliated director was therefore to serve on each of three standing committees—nominating, compensation, and audit.

Although responsible for operation of the PJM control area, Services was to perform specific services as an *agent* for parties to the TOA, MOA, and RSA subject to agreed performance criteria, all as set forth in the ISOA. Under the ISOA the transmission owners granted the ISO a continuing *license* to use the facilities and equipment previously used by the PJMIA.[21]

On behalf of the parties to the TOA, Services was to:

- operate the PJM control area
- direct and coordinate operation of high-voltage transmission facilities
- administer the PJM tariff

- administer a protocol for regional transmission expansion planning and develop such a plan
- coordinate planned outages
- promulgate directives and guidelines for operation of transmission facilities
- perform reliability studies
- operate the PJM OASIS

On behalf of the parties to the MOA, Services was to:

- commit, schedule, and dispatch generating resources within the PJM control area
- account for transactions
- receive and disburse transaction revenues
- conduct compliance monitoring

On behalf of the parties to the RSA, Services was to:

- perform calculations necessary to determine overall reserve requirement and its allocation to individual parties
- conduct compliance monitoring
- receive and disburse charges imposed under the RSA
- perform required data collection

Services' annual operating budget reflected the foregoing allocation of responsibilities. Funding obligations were initially to be borne by the parties to the TOA, MOA, and RSA to the extent of 41%, 48%, and 11%, respectively, but the transmission owners alone were to fund Services' working capital requirements.[22]

Services were subject to removal as ISO by administrative committees appointed under the TOA, MOA, and RSA if it failed to perform satisfactorily or committed a willful violation of the ISOA.[23] The transmission owners thus retained ultimate control. Services' autonomy, although sufficient "to mitigate any market power of the PJM members,"[24] did not mean that "it should be insulated from meaningful standards of performance or that the parties relying on it as the independent system operator should be prohibited from replacing it to satisfy those standards."[25] Order No. 888 was cited as authority for the proposition that "transmission owners need to be able to hold the ISO accountable for its fiduciary role . . ."[26] In addition to their power of removal, the transmission owners could terminate the ISOA, and thus the ISO's agency relationship, simply by terminating the TOA.[27] Upon the ISO's termination or resignation, the transmission owners, through the administrative committees, were empowered to select a successor ISO.[28]

PJM Dispute Resolution Agreement

The ISO and each of the parties to the TOA, the MOA, and the RSA were all to be parties to the PJM Dispute Resolution Agreement (DRA), which contemplated good faith negotiations to resolve differences, non-binding mediation, and binding arbitration for monetary disputes in which the amount in controversy is $1 million or less. The DRA was not intended to displace dispute resolution provisions in the PJM tariff.

FERC Order

On November 13, 1996 FERC issued an order rejecting PJM's restructuring plan as filed.[29] FERC measured the plan against Order No. 888 and found that the proposed ISO did not comport with its principles, the proposed PJM tariff failed to meet its non-discriminatory open access requirements, and the proposed agreements did not embody the power pool reforms it contemplated.

ISO

Given the extent of the transmission owners' retained control and proposed governance structure, it is not surprising that FERC found the proposed ISO to lack independence and preclude meaningful representation by non-PJM stakeholders. FERC objected to the presence of affiliated directors and the extent of oversight by administrative committees dominated by transmission owner representatives since the committees, FERC noted, could establish the need for transmission expansion, develop operating procedures, and determine reserve obligations. The ISO's resulting lack of independence was deemed to be a fundamental flaw in PJM's proposal.

FERC also expressed concern about other features of PJM's proposal in relation to Order No. 888's ISO criteria:

- transmission owners' control over the ISO's budget and possible ability to influence the ISO's employees through transferred stock plans and pension benefits
- the network transmission service tariff's use of zonal pricing (except as a transitional means to mitigate cost-shifting), its imposition of a 10% surcharge when resources are imported from outside a zone, inapplicability of tariff rates to transmission owners' resources, and unavailability of point-to-point service for transactions into or out of the PJM control area[30]
- vesting of primary responsibility for planning and reliability in administrative committees dominated by transmission owners rather than in the ISO itself
- lack of clarity regarding which facilities the ISO would control and for which it would be responsible in its capacity as tariff administrator
- impact of locational marginal pricing on system constraints, payment of congestion charges, and crediting of such charges to the holders of firm transmission rights
- lack of appropriate incentives to induce efficient management and administration of the ISO
- impact of transmission pricing on short-run dispatch and consumption decisions, expansion of the grid by non-PJM members and development of a secondary market in tradable capacity rights

TOA, MOA, RSA, and ISOA

In FERC's view the proposal's array of interrelated agreements and committees concentrated voting rights in the hands of the transmission owners, thereby precluding "others from having any meaningful influence over any aspect of the proposed Mid-Atlantic Market . . . [and] perpetuat[ing] the control of the PJM pool by the [PJM] Companies."[31]

The result, FERC concluded, would be unduly discriminatory membership and operation of the power pool. FERC directed the PJM companies to file amended agreements by December 31, 1996. In so doing, FERC required that all stakeholders participate in formation of the ISO; that the PJM board represent all stakeholders or no stakeholders, *i.e.,* that it be a representative or fully independent board; that administrative committees' control over the ISO be moderated and made subject to commission review; that the ISO develop its own operating procedures and perform long-range transmission planning, and that the PJM tariff not discriminate between classes of customers and otherwise comport fully with the provisions of FERC's *pro forma* tariff.

Further procedural steps

As noted, PECO Energy, a PJM company, had withdrawn from the majority's filing and submitted its own countervailing restructuring proposal. Although FERC had also rejected PECO's proposal, that rejection did not materially diminish the differences between the parties. As a result, the majority had but a few weeks to enter into negotiations with stakeholders, attempt to accommodate its differences with PECO, and reframe a unitary filing at FERC in accordance with the November order. After that filing, the parties anticipated development of a definitive restructuring proposal to be filed at FERC by May 31, 1997.

Following several meetings with stakeholders in December 1996, the PJM companies were able to reach agreement on most issues relating to implementation of the *pro forma* tariff. PECO and the PJM companies nonetheless remained divided on two critical matters impacting regional transmission service:

- whether zonal rates or a single pool-wide rate should be used for network integration service
- the methodology for addressing transmission congestion

To reflect the parties' differences in a unitary submission, the filing documents contained alternative proposals, which were made subject to FERC guidance, a so-called jump ball approach.[32]

Pending resolution of open matters and FERC authorization of an ISO, PJM's Office of the Interconnection (OI) was to continue to administer the pool on a day-to-day basis[33]and to report to a newly created independent eight-member board, representing all market participants and including the president of the OI as a non-voting *ex officio* member. The board members were to have relevant utility and commercial market expertise but no business relationship with the transmission owners. The board was to be elected by a sectoral Management Committee, representing generation owners, transmission owners, wholesale system users, retail system users and other suppliers.[34] Following such election, however, the Management Committee's role was to be advisory only.

As proposed in the December 31 filing, the energy market was to be a bid-based market. Generation located in the control area would be bid at cost. The OI was to operate an hourly spot market into which all generators could bid their energy and from which all buyers could purchase energy. Market participants would also be free to arrange bilateral energy transactions or to self-schedule their own generation. Bids for generation located outside the PJM control area would be cost-based unless the entity submitting the bid had market-based pricing authority.

The PJM tariff and restructuring changes reflected in the December 31 filing represented an interim solution reflecting numerous compromises, acceptable to the parties only on a short-term basis. It was clear that a definitive solution would require a continuing restructuring process and additional stakeholder consultation in order to establish an ISO approved by FERC. The PJM companies assured the Commission that the management committee would not control that process and that the board would "have no authority to address any market restructuring issues, including the handling of congestion pricing or any other areas of disagreement . . ."[35]

PJM Tariff

The PJM tariff submitted as part of the December 31 filing was intended to provide pool-wide open access transmission service on a comparable basis throughout and across the pool for all energy and capacity transactions. In comparison to FERC's *pro forma* tariff, however, the PJM tariff reflected:

- changes to reflect regional practices and the fact that the tariff would apply to a group of companies, *i.e.,* a pool, and not simply to a single transmission provider
- changes to implement alternative rate designs for Network Integration Transmission Service
- changes to implement alternative methods for dealing with re-dispatch resulting from transmission congestion

The changes also reflected alternative, side-by-side provisions propounded by PECO and the PJM companies, as to which the parties could not reach agreement.[36]

As administrator of the PJM tariff, the OI was to provide transmission service using the PJM companies' facilities. All firm transmission users, including transmission owners, would then pay a single, non-pancaked transmission rate based on the costs of the transmission system where the point of delivery is located.[37] Firm transmission customers and transmission owners (on behalf of native load) were to reserve firm points of receipt and delivery. Non-firm transmission customers were also to pay a single, non-pancaked transmission service rate.

Unlike PECO, which proposed to recover congestion costs from all pool users as a general uplift charge, the PJM companies contemplated recovery of congestion costs from the parties transacting on the congested path, using locational marginal pricing to determine such costs. To hedge against incurrence of congestion costs, the PJM companies also proposed that all firm customers be awarded fixed transmission rights (FTRs) for specific receipt and delivery point reservations. Users with firm reservations would then hedge against congestion charges by scheduling transactions consistent with the points of receipt and delivery specified in their reservations. Network customers and transmission owners would hedge against congestion costs by nominating that portion of their network resources serving the load in respect of which they had received FTRs. Any other use of the transmission system by a firm customer would be subject to congestion charges during a period of constrained transmission capacity, *i.e.*, when a firm point-to-point customer uses secondary receipt and delivery points, when a network customer or transmission owner schedules energy from a non-network resource, and when a network customer or transmission owner schedules energy from a network resource for which it has not nominated FTRs (Fig. 3-4).

A Fixed Transmission Right (FTR) is a financial instrument that entitles the holder to receive compensation for transmission congestion charges that arise when the transmission grid is congested in the day-ahead market and differences in day-ahead locational marginal prices (LMPs) result from the dispatch of generators out of merit order to relieve the congestion. Each FTR is defined from a point of receipt (where the power is injected onto the PJM grid) to a point of delivery (where the power is withdrawn from the PJM grid). For each hour in which congestion exists on the transmission system between the receipt and delivery points specified in the FTR, the holder of the FTR is awarded a share of the transmission congestion charges collected from the market participants.

FTRs are available to all PJM firm transmission service customers (Network Integration Service or Firm Point-to-Point Service), since these customers pay the embedded cost of the PJM Transmission System. The purpose of FTRs is to protect firm transmission service customers from increased cost due to transmission congestion when their energy deliveries are consistent with their firm reservations. Essentially, FTRs are financial entitlements to rebates of congestion charges paid by the firm transmission service customers. They do not represent a right to physical delivery of power.

The holder of the FTR is not required to deliver energy in order to receive a congestion credit. If a constraint exists on the transmission system, the holders of FTRs receive a credit based on the FTR MW reservation and the LMP difference between point of delivery and point of receipt. This credit is paid to the holder regardless of who delivered energy or the amount delivered across the path designated in the FTR.

Fig. 3–4 Definition and Purpose of FTRs

To reflect the regional nature of transmission service, the PJM companies proposed that network resources and loads be integrated over the eight utility systems and a single transmission service rate be assessed for each firm reservation, no matter how many constituent systems may be involved in providing transmission. The PJM tariff also proposed changes to the point-to-point rate design by establishing a single point-to-point rate for delivery points in each zone.

FERC's interim order

On February 28, 1997 FERC issued an order that accepted the parties' filing effective March 1, 1997.[38] The order directed PJM to implement PECO's transmission congestion pricing proposal, subject to refund, but supported the PJM companies on all other issues.[39] The order also confirmed the Commission's intention to convene a technical conference to explore resolution of issues not fully addressed in the filing.

Transformation of PJM

It soon became apparent that the OI could no longer function effectively as an unincorporated association—its legal status since 1993. The candidates selected for the OI's board feared exposure to legal liability and declined to serve in a directorial capacity until organizational changes were made. After considering several alternative possibilities, the PJM companies therefore submitted to stakeholders for approval a limited liability company (LLC) as the instrumentality of choice and a draft operating agreement (OA), adapting certain provisions of the existing PJM Interconnection Agreement, as its organic document. Prior to FERC's review, the PJM companies proposed to organize the LLC and cause its board of managers to be elected by the LLC's members, including initially all the former members of the PJM power pool.[40] Accordingly, on March 31, 1997, PJM Interconnection Association, an unincorporated association, was converted into PJM Interconnection, LLC under the applicable provisions of the Delaware Limited Liability Company Act.[41] All of PJM Interconnection Association's assets and liabilities were transferred to and assumed by the LLC by operation of law.[42]

On April 1, 1997, on behalf of its members, the LLC filed the OA with FERC as a replacement for the PJM Interconnection Agreement previously submitted in connection with the December 31 filing to become effective on March 1, 1997. In its transmittal letter the LLC stated "conversion from an unincorporated association to a limited liability company format does not affect the transmission, market operations or governance provisions that were filed December 31, 1996." The LLC requested that the OA become effective as of March 31, 1997, "contemporaneously with the start of service under the pool-wide open access transmission tariff." The bid-based energy market commenced at the same time.

Operating Agreement

As its name implies, the OA is a LLC's controlling legal document. Upon its filing with FERC on April 1, 1997, the OA was characterized as the successor to the original PJM Agreement, *i.e.,* the PJM Interconnection Agreement tracing its origin to the early days of the PJM power pool, "pending determination, regulatory approval and implementation of permanent restructuring . . ."[43]

As set forth in the OA, LLC had as its principal purpose "the operation of the Interconnection in accordance with this Agreement and the other agreements and arrangements between the LLC and one or more Members."[44] In recognition of its then interim status, the term of the LLC was to continue only until the OA was replaced by a definitive restructuring agreement approved by FERC or December 31, 1997, unless extended by members holding two-thirds of the membership interests in the LLC.[45]

The OA's other salient features were as follows:

- It defined the OI as the "facilities and staff of the LLC engaged in implementation of [the OA] and administration of the Tariff."[46] The OA thus implicitly treated the OI as the incipient ISO, although the OI was simply an aggregation of existing personnel and administrative functions within the LLC, not a separate legal entity with specified powers.

- It imposed on the OI the responsibility to raise working capital through non-recourse financing up to $5.2 million, failing which the LLC's members, *i.e.,* initially the transmission owners, would contribute working capital up to that amount in proportion to their weighted interests.[47]

- It created a sectorial management committee with sectorial voting power, including power to elect the PJM board, composed of members' representatives.[48] The management committee was to advise the PJM board on forecast requirements for electric generating capacity and operating reserve capacity.[49]

- It authorized an LLC board of managers (the PJM board), elected by the management committee from a slate of candidates proposed by an independent consultant, with authority for supervision and administration of all matters pertaining to the Interconnection and the LLC. Significantly, the PJM board was to perform these duties "in a manner consistent with the creation and operation of a robust, competitive and non-discriminatory electric power market in the PJM control area and so that no member or group of members will have undue influence over the operation of the interconnection."[50] However, the PJM board was to have "no authority to address or implement a restructuring or other reorganization of the Interconnection of the LLC."[51] The seven outside board members were required to have expertise and experience in defined areas.[52]

- It provided for the PJM board's appointment of a president to direct and manage the day-to-day operation of the LLC, including operating, planning, coordination, interchange accounting, and other related functions.[53]

- It established transmission owner rights, not subject to modification or limitation by the PJM board or the management committee, including the right of the transmission owners to file unilaterally for changes in rates, terms and conditions of transmission services, including amendment of the PJM tariff, pursuant to Section 205 of the FPA and the right of any transmission owner to withdraw from the OA.[54]

- It specified that members "shall not take part in the management of the business nor transact any business for the LLC in their capacity as Members . . ."[55] At the same time, it accorded the members a limited property interest in the LLC upon its liquidation and to recover capital contributed to the LLC.[56]

After further consideration of the OA as submitted and before accepting office, the nominees to the PJM board sought clarification of their role, including the right to serve on the governing board of the eventual ISO. The nominees also required certain changes in the OA, to which the management committee acquiesced. On April 25, 1997 PJM filed amendments to the OA with FERC.

The amendments restated the primary responsibility of the PJM board to include "safe and reliable operation of the Interconnection," deleted the provision denying the PJM board authority to address or implement restructuring of the Interconnection or the LLC,[57] and made amendment or alteration of the OA dependent on "acceptance and/or approval by FERC, as may be required by law."[58] The amendments also gave notice that the PJM board would insist on its independence. In a schedule to the OA, the PJM board was accorded the "right to provide information in restructuring negotiations and related regulatory proceedings" and the right to "argue in favor of any restructuring proposal, including Board composition or membership." In addition, individual members of the PJM board were assured the opportunity to continue to serve on the board of a successor ISO.[59]

Technical conference

On April 9, 1997 FERC announced a technical conference to address the PJM companies' and PECO's respective congestion management and pricing proposals. FERC had previously deferred the PJM companies' locational marginal pricing/fixed transmission rights proposal pending further review. It had also propounded detailed questions about the proposal, to which PJM filed a response[60] describing the proposal's essential features.

At the conference Philip G. Harris, PJM's president and chief executive officer, addressed the scope of PJM's operations and its technical preparations to implement either of the congestion management and pricing proposals. His description of PJM's operating environment emphasized its complexity:

The transmission system is dynamic and requires continual monitoring and anticipation of events in order to avoid potential problems, the most serious being the loss of customer demand or load. The PJM Energy Management System (EMS), which is central to our real time operations, receives over 10,000 telemetered data items every 14 seconds, and an additional 5,300 values, which are transferred to the PJM EMS each, time their status changes. Every 30 seconds, a System Security program reviews all 663 monitored transmission facilities to ensure that they are within established reliability limits. Additionally, 150 other points are monitored for sudden changes due to voltage, generation or frequency events. Every 10 minutes, each of the 663 monitored transmission facilities [is] analyzed for the contingency impact of losing each of the transmission lines, transformers, and generators in the system model. The most severe contingency on every single transmission facility is then compared to its emergency and normal thermal rating, with results reported to the system operator. Over 450,000 potential system problems are analyzed each 10 minutes. On-line State Estimation and Power Flow programs are also run every 10 minutes to identify reactive limitations, with results again reported to the system operator. The system operator also has current information that identifies the impact of every generating unit and phase angle regulator on each transmission line's actual flow and postulated contingency flow. This information serves as the basis for any remedial action that must be taken, based on reports provided from the monitoring program . . .[61] (Fig. 3-5)

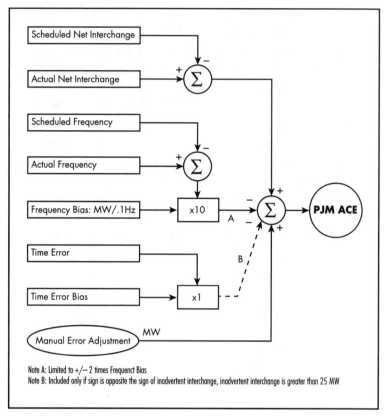

Fig. 3-5 Calculation of PJM Area Control Error (ACE)

Notwithstanding this complexity, Mr. Harris concluded that locational marginal pricing methodology could be implemented according to the PJM companies' plan.

The June 2, 1997 filing

Although the December 31 and April 1 filings provided for expanded participation in the PJM pool and enhanced the independence of the PJM pool operator, they did not purport to establish an ISO. In the June 2 filing, by contrast, the PJM companies modified the governance provisions of the

OA to ensure that the OI, subject to the oversight of the PJM board, would independently administer the day-to-day operations of the PJM pool in accordance with the ISO criteria set forth in Order No. 888. The June 2 filing did not characterize either the OI or the related LLC as a public utility.[62]

The revised governance provisions were a direct result of discussions among the PJM companies and other stakeholders. As revised, the OA was intended to establish an ISO with responsibility for system operations, administration of the PJM tariff and regional transmission planning, subject to a governing board independent of any market participant and seized of complete responsibility for supervision and oversight of day-to-day operations.

To preserve PJM's assurance of power supply reliability, the provisions formerly contained in the OA relating to long-term power supply planning were transferred to a reliability assurance agreement among the PJM control area load-serving entities and modified to accommodate the impending introduction of retail choice.

An expanded and clarified explanation of LMP was incorporated as Attachment K to the PJM tariff, which specified that both users of network service and firm point-to-point service would receive FTRs and allocated any excess transmission congestion charges to the OI.[63] Under LMP the spot price of transmission was said to be derived directly from the difference in spot prices for energy at the withdrawal and injection locations for which transmission service is provided with the result that the prices of transmission and energy—and their respective markets—are conceptually linked. The filing also proposed to implement "up to" rates for non-firm point-to-point transmission services, and to charge the higher of congestion costs (based on locational price differences between points of receipt and delivery) and the embedded cost rate if a non-firm point-to-point customer chooses to wheel through congestion rather than be interrupted.

The filing emphasized continuity with PJM's historic pattern of operation, particularly realization of energy cost savings through regional economic dispatch. It noted the ISO would operate a voluntary hourly spot market, with transparent market prices, into which all generators have the option to bid their energy and from which all buyers have the option to purchase their energy. These features were deemed to preserve a primary benefit of a tight power pool while according market participants flexibility in arranging transactions and maximizing the efficient use of generation and transmission.

Operating Agreement

As revised, the OA reflected the following features:

- organizational transformation of the former unincorporated association to a limited liability company with an independent board of managers, elected by a members committee, responsible for supervision and oversight of the day-to-day operations of the pool
- confirmation that the PJM board's primary responsibility is to ensure that the ISO's functions are accomplished in a manner consistent with the safe and reliable operation of the interconnection, creation of and operation of a robust, competitive, and non-discriminatory electric power market in the PJM control area, and the principle that members shall not have undue influence over operation of the Interconnection
- formation of a sectorial members committee including generation owners, other suppliers, transmission owners, electric distributors, and end-use customers
- voting provisions for the members committee ensuring that no sector can control or veto action by the members committee
- creation of users groups to focus environmental and public interest concerns
- clear delineation of the respective roles of the PJM board, the Office of the Interconnection, and the members committee so that the Office of the Interconnection controls day-to-day operations of the PJM control area and the PJM interchange energy market, administers the PJM tariff and transmission expansion planning protocol, and performs the data collection and analysis necessary for reserve sharing. The PJM board is the governance structure that supervises the Office of the Interconnection. The Members Committee elects the PJM board, has the power to amend or terminate the OA, and provides advice and recommendations to the PJM board and the Office of the Interconnection

- clear delineation of members' rights and obligations, including an obligation to comply with NERC, MAAC and other reliability standards and to respond to emergency directives of the Office of the Interconnection
- administration by the Office of the Interconnection of a pool spot energy market coupled with the least-cost, security-constrained commitment and dispatch of generating resources to serve load in the control area

The filing also noted two pending refinements to the pool energy market:

- a multi-settlement system allowing market participants to commit and obtain commitments to energy prices and transmission congestion charges at specified deadlines in advance of real-time dispatch[64]
- an auction of FTRs to permit market participants to obtain FTRs in addition to those retained by network and point-to-point transmission customers (including those taking service under bilateral contracts) as a hedge against congestion charges[65]

Transmission Owners Agreement

Under the transmission owners agreement (TOA) the transmission owners agreed to provide regional transmission service using non-pancaked rates pursuant to the PJM tariff and to transfer to the ISO responsibility for administration of the PJM tariff and regional planning and operations.

The TOA created an administrative committee of transmission owners with advisory functions but expressly denied them the right to exercise any control over the ISO. The TOA also limited the transmission owners' right to file proposed changes in transmission service rate design and non-rate terms and conditions under Section 205 of the FPA to those changes not rejected by a majority of the PJM board. If proposed changes are so rejected, the filing must be made instead under Section 206 of the FPA. The TOA nonetheless reserved to the transmission owners the right to assure recovery of their revenue requirements and other related rights claimed in the December 31 filing.

PJM Tariff

As submitted, the PJM tariff implemented LMP for transmission congestion but contemplated no changes to the underlying revenue requirements or increases in pool-wide rates. To facilitate retail choice, the PJM tariff altered the demand calculation for network service from a 12-month rolling average load ratio share calculation to a stated rate per MW-year applied to actual loads of the network customer in a month.[66]

The PJM companies also proposed one point-to-point rate for delivery points at the border of the control area and separate point-to-point rates for delivery points in each zone, although pool-wide transmission service was still to be available at a single, non-pancaked rate. All transmission service—whether network or point-to-point—to loads within a zone would have the same rate per MW-year.

Reliability Assurance Agreement

The Reliability Assurance Agreement (RAA), successor to the Reserve Sharing Agreement, required transmission owners and other load-serving entities within the PJM control area to serve loads therein, provide assistance during emergencies, and coordinate the planning of capacity resources, while delegating all day-to-day functions to the Office of the Interconnection (including admission of new parties and the data collection, analyses, calculations, and monitoring necessary to implement the agreement).

To do this the RAA:

- retained a two-year ahead forecast of capacity needs (the forecast pool requirement)[67]
- provided a transition from a two-year to a three-month advance commitment of load-serving entities to satisfy their share of forecast capacity needs
- changed from an annual to a monthly allocation of each load-serving entity's capacity requirement

- relied on the Office of the Interconnection to perform key tasks, including the screening of potential parties to the agreement, calculation of requirements imposed by the agreement and monitoring of parties' compliance with those requirements (Fig. 3-6)

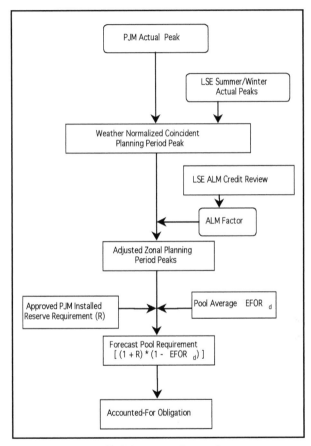

Fig. 3–6 Installed Capacity System Requirements

To mitigate shifts in capacity obligations, the RAA relied on zones coextensive with the service territories of the PJM companies until the date when all states within the PJM control area have adopted retail access programs for end-use electric customers and more than 85% of such customers had a choice of electric supplier.

The RAA's zones were to be used to determine the obligation to plan and commit for future capacity resources (the forecast LSE requirement) and the obligation to have the resources in place during the planning period (the accounted for obligation). Prior to the pool-wide choice date, the forecast LSE requirement would be determined by first allocating the forecast pool requirement to each of the zones based on the forecast of load for the zone (the forecast zone requirement), subject to further allocation to the parties serving loads within the zone based on forecast of loads. After the pool-wide choice date, the forecast LSE requirement of a party would then be determined by allocating the forecast pool requirement directly to the parties based on their forecasts of loads.

Compliance with ISO criteria

To confirm that PJM qualified as an ISO, the PJM companies included in their filing a brief evaluating PJM in view of the ISO principles FERC had set forth in Order No. 888.[68] The brief identified the PJM's independent board of managers, the Office of the Interconnection charged with day-to-day operational responsibility and the policy setting, but advisory members committee as essential elements. The PJM board was said to "ensure that the Office of Interconnection can perform its operating responsibilities without undue influence from the Members, individually or as a whole."[69] Specifically, the brief noted, the PJM board was to have the right to propose amendments to the OA, oppose Section 205 and 206 filings by members, submit its own independent comments to regulators, and establish capital and operating budgets for PJM.[70]

The brief also noted that the Office of the Interconnection would maintain PJM's historic operation of its interconnected transmission facilities as a single control area, subject to the OA, which was said to have "transformed the PJM interconnection association office into the Office of the Interconnection as the operating arm of an independent system operator."[71] The Office of the Interconnection's operating prerogatives were also described as bringing forward its predecessor's long-standing authority and ability to dispatch generation out of merit order as necessary to alleviate constraints on the transmission system in the PJM control area, thereafter using prices of generation under its dispatch to establish locational marginal prices for energy, with transmission costs established by the differences in locational marginal prices caused by transmission congestion. The brief characterized LMP, established by the OA, as a comprehensive set of trading rules governing energy pricing, management of transmission congestion, and a competitive energy market.

Comments of the PJM board

Exercising its right to speak independently, the PJM board filed comments on the PJM companies' proposal.[72]

As the governing body of a limited liability company (LLC), the PJM board noted, it enjoyed only those rights conferred on it by the OA; and by unilaterally amending or terminating the OA or collateral agreements tied to it such as the TOA or the RAA, the PJM companies could implicitly control the PJM board. For example, the PJM board noted that the transmission owners retained the right to terminate or amend the TOA, under which the parties had delegated to PJM and the PJM board, in accordance with the OA, the responsibility to direct operation of their transmission facilities and responsibility for administering the PJM tariff. Termination of the TOA would therefore necessarily terminate its operational delegation of responsibility, and the power to amend the TOA therefore implied the power to alter as well as terminate that delegation. Similarly, load-serving entities retained the power to amend, terminate, or withdraw from the RAA upon notice to PJM and concurrent withdrawal from the OA. That power was deemed significant given the RAA's delegation of important reliability functions to PJM and the PJM board.

The PJM board insisted accordingly on due process rights to object to any proposed amendments to or termination of the OA, the TOA, and the RAA. Specifically, the PJM board contended that any proposed termination or amendment of the referenced agreements must be the subject of a noticed filing requiring FERC approval. If the PJM board were then to object to or protest termination or amendment, it would have a forum in which to be heard. FERC oversight would prevent members from unilaterally asserting amendment or termination rights in an effort to control the PJM board and the ISO.

The PJM board also expressed concern about the OA's establishment of a Finance Committee, controlled by representatives of the Members Committee and parties to the TOA and the RAA, to which PJM was required to submit annual budgets for review. Only following the Finance Committee's analysis and recommendations would the PJM board adopt operating and capital budgets for the LLC. This arrangement suggested that the members could through the Finance Committee attempt to influence the PJM board, which they have the power to elect and reelect, by using the budgetary process to advance, delay, or influence activities affecting the interests of a particular party or sector. The PJM board viewed the Finance Committee's role as solely advisory.[73] To remove any question of self-serving influence or control, however, the PJM board urged FERC to consider ordering an independent self-funding structure to be adopted by the LLC for recovery of the costs of its jurisdictional services.

The PJM board's comments also confirmed its understanding of the nomination and election process, under which an independent consultant selects a slate of candidates for election by the members, asserting that the nominated slate of candidates may consist of one or more candidates to fill any available position. Incumbent PJM board members may stand for reelection, and the members may not compel selection of a favored consultant to propose nominees for election.

The PJM board took note of the fact that both the TOA and the RAA transfer significant ISO-related responsibilities to the Office of the Interconnection rather than to the LLC. As described in the OA, however, the Office of the Interconnection was deemed to be nothing more than "the employees and agents of the LLC engaged in implementation of [the OA] and administration of the PJM tariff, subject to the supervision and oversight of the PJM Board . . ."[74] In short, the PJM board observed, the Office of the Interconnection is not a legal entity, lacks legal capacity, and is simply a constituent element of the LLC. Within this hybrid structure, the PJM board said the Office of the Interconnection would discharge ISO functions, including implementation of the OA and administration of the PJM tariff, but could do so only as an agent for others. To address this concern, the PJM board interpreted references to the Office of the Interconnection to include all actions taken on behalf of the LLC, subject to supervision and oversight of the PJM board when required to discharge ISO functions.

Dispute resolution also came under scrutiny. As filed, the TOA subjected disputes between transmission owners and the LLC to resolution by the TOA administrative committee rather than a disinterested panel or neutral arbitral body. The PJM board suggested substitution of an impartial procedure to govern disputes between a party to the TOA and the LLC.

"Precisely defining the role of PJM in these filed agreements," the PJM board concluded, "is particularly important because the underlying legal vehicle is a limited liability company, not a traditional corporation. Under Delaware law, a limited liability company can provide a board of managers with as little or as much authority as the parties intend depending in large measure upon the terms of the relevant agreements."[75]

PJM interchange energy market

The PJM interchange energy market (PX) became operational on April 1, 1997[76] and continued as an integral feature of the PJM restructuring proposal under which energy and related services were offered at cost-based rates, prospectively subject to Schedule 1 of the amended OA submitted as part of the June 2 filing. In a further filing on July 14, 1997 the PJM companies requested FERC authorization to make market-based offers for sales through the PX.[77] In support of their request, the PJM companies contended they would not be able to exercise market power in the principal relevant geographical and product markets and proposed mitigation measures to eliminate any residual market power concerns.

Under the proposed arrangements sellers of energy through the PX would provide the ISO information on prices and amounts of energy offered on a day-ahead basis.[78] Entities serving load within the PJM control area would then provide information concerning bilateral or self-scheduled arrangements, *i.e.,* arrangements used directly to serve their own load in lieu of trading through the pool. On a day-ahead basis, those serving load would also provide the ISO estimates of load to be served through the PX and quantities of bilateral purchases. Entities outside the PJM control area who wish to purchase energy from the PX would provide estimates of hourly quantities and price levels above which they do not wish to purchase.

The ISO would then use the bid price, actual load and generation data, together with information on transmission limits and the operational characteristics of the generators submitting bids to dispatch the system. The dispatch results would be used to compute marginal cost at each load and generator location. These node-specific marginal costs would define the prices at which energy is bought and sold in the PX. While the sellers would provide their bids on a day-ahead basis, dispatch would be accomplished on a real-time basis with marginal costs calculated every five minutes. When averaged for each hour, such marginal costs would form the basis for payments to sellers and payments from customers. Marginal costs would differ by location as a result of line losses and congestion on the transmission system[79] (Fig. 3-7).

To support the filing, the PJM companies submitted *Report on Horizontal Market Power Analysis*. The report found, in the near term, that the bulk of the purchasing activity in the PX would be attributable to vertically integrated utilities with sufficient generating resources to meet their own requirements if prices rise above competitive levels. The opportunities for self-supply would therefore constrain the ability of generation suppliers to exercise market power.[80]

In fact, the weighted average price of electricity in PJM's spot market largely remained within a band ranging from $20 to $50 per Mwh between 1997 and 2001.

The report also addressed market-based ancillary services to be provided by the ISO including energy imbalance service, regulation, spinning reserves, and operating reserves.[81]

Energy imbalance service. Under the PJM tariff energy imbalance service is provided when a difference occurs between the scheduled and the actual delivery of energy to a load located within the control area over a single hour. Payments for the service are tied to the PX price and are not thought to present market power concerns.

Regulation. Raising or lowering the output of on-line generators to follow moment-to-moment changes in load provides regulation. To provide this service, PJM imposes a pool regulation requirement equal to 1.1% of daily peak load, allocated among load-serving entities in proportion to their peak demands. The requirement may be met through self-supply or purchase from other generators located within the PJM control area at the market-clearing price of energy. Since the PJM control area requires only small quantities of regulation service, generators are deemed to lack incentive to distort bidding behavior in the energy market to obtain higher prices.[82]

Spinning and operating reserves. Operating reserves include spinning reserves, 10-minute reserves, and 30-minute reserves. Spinning reserves are required to serve load immediately in the event of a contingency and are provided from the unloaded capability of generating units currently on-line and synchronized to the system. The PJM control area must have sufficient spinning reserves at all times to allow recovery from the largest single contingency anticipated—*e.g.*, the loss of a large nuclear unit of more than 1,000 MW—and to be able to restore its schedules on external ties within 10 minutes. The amount of spinning reserve capability of any individual generator is thus the difference between its current operating level, if on-line, and the level it could reach in 10 minutes. PJM's requirement for 10-minute reserves is approximately 1,700 MW. PJM also provides for 10-minute and 30-minute reserves, provided by the unloaded portion of on-line generating units and quick start generation, equal (together with spinning reserves) to 10% of forecast daily peak load. Operating reserve requirements are calculated based upon probabilities and depending on the expected load forecast inaccuracy and generation mix.

To provide operating reserves, generators submit bids on a daily basis to the ISO. Bids include start-up and no load costs, multiple energy blocks and an offer to provide regulation. The ISO uses this bid information and information on generator ramp rates, self-scheduled generation and loads to dispatch the system in economic fashion in view of reliability considerations and transmission constraints. In so doing, it determines which generators to schedule and, for each, the amount of energy and reserves it is to supply during each time block. For each unit scheduled, the value of its energy output (*i.e.*, the prevailing spot price times the quantity of energy supplied) is compared to the sum of its start up and no load costs plus its energy bid prices for the output actually produced. Generators are then credited for any amount by which their energy value falls short of the sum of their start up, no load, and energy bid prices. The sum of such credits paid to all generators is deemed to be the cost of operating reserves, which is then recovered from pool participants in proportion to their control area load.[83] Operating reserves, so defined, represent a residual form of payment for generators whose start-up and no load costs would otherwise be less than fully compensated through energy payment rather than a type of generation service required to ensure system reliability.[84]

Notes

[1] Under Order No. 888 and Section 35.38(c)(3) of FERC's regulations, 18 C.F.R. § 35.28 (c)(3), tight power pools, such as PJM, were required to file and take service under joint pool-wide *pro forma* open access non-discriminatory transmission tariffs and reformed pooling agreements not later than December 31, 1996. The reformed power pooling agreements were required to establish open, non-discriminatory membership provisions, including establishment of an ISO if chosen as the pool's preferred method of remedying undue discrimination

[2] Section 6.6.1 of the transmission owners agreement (TOA) gave the transmission owners the unilateral right to make an application to FERC for a change, other than a change in a zonal rate, in "any rate, change, charge, term and condition, classification or service, or any rule or regulation related thereto, under Section 205 of the Federal Power Act . . ." Subsequently, after FERC had recognized PJM as an ISO, it sought and obtained authority to make tariff changes unilaterally, *i.e.,* without the concurrence or prior approval of the transmission owners

[3] *Open Access Same-Time Information System,* Final Rule, Order No. 889, III FERC Stats. & Regs. ¶ 31,035 (1996) (hereafter *Order No. 889)*

[4] Other criteria for party status are set forth in Article 3 of the TOA and include conformity with FERC, NERC, MAAC, and Good Utility Practices principles, guidelines, standards and requirements. In addition, incorporation of an additional party's transmission facilities within the PJM control area must be "without material adverse impact on the cost or reliability of transmission service" by then existing parties to the TOA

[5] *Restructuring of the Pennsylvania-New Jersey-Maryland Interconnection,* at 4, Docket Nos. EC96-28-000, EL96-69-000, and ER96-2516-000 (July 24, 1996) (hereafter "July 4, 1996 Application")

[6] 7/24/96 application; mimeo, p. 6

[7] The PJM utilities contended, to the contrary, that the "rate design will ensure that all loads within a transmission zone, including the native load customers of transmission owners, will be responsible for comparable shares of the transmission revenue requirements. As a result, similarly situated suppliers competing to serve a load will be indifferent to the network transmission rate." (July 24, 1996 Application, p. 9) Because all network customers within a zone pay the same rate, the differences between zones were not thought to compromise compliance with the comparability requirement

[8] As set forth in Appendix A to Schedule 1 of the Mid-Atlantic Market Operations Agreement, one of the platform agreements forming the basis of PJM's initial ISO filing at FERC, the ISO calculates the locational marginal price (LMP) for each load bus and generation bus included in the ISO's power flow model for the PJM control area. LMP is calculated using linear programming techniques, applied to the output of the solved power flow model employed by the ISO (referred to as the state estimator) and the generation price information submitted by market sellers. Using the state estimator output, the LMP program determines the marginal cost to serve load at each bus, as reflected in the market seller's offers, based on the load requirements at each bus and the location of the bus with respect to transmission limits. The marginal cost so derived is the LMP for the bus. The state estimator program provides generator values, bus loads, distribution factors for line sensitivity, and transmission limits—all as reflected in a solved power flow case. The prices offered by market sellers provide incremental price curves for generating units. The ISO dispatcher provides current dispatch rates (the hourly rate being used for dispatch of combustion turbines) and transmission limits and specifies the generating units to be dispatched out of economic merit order as a result of transmission limits. The LMP program is operated at five minute intervals, based on the last completed state estimator solution. A LMP for each bus is calculated every five minutes and the results averaged (weighted by MW) over each one-hour period to determine charges to market buyers, credits to market sellers, and transmission congestion charges

[9] By order issued July 18, 1997 in Docket No. ER97-3463-000, FERC granted PJM's request to eliminate tariff provisions allowing re-dispatch of generating resources for non-firm transmission service willing to pay congestion charges. In implementing the re-dispatch provisions, PJM found that economic dispatch within the PJM power pool was being adversely affected. Network customers, not fully compensated under the PJM tariff for their re-dispatch costs, self-scheduled their units rather than submitting them to the pool's economic dispatch. As a result, PJM found that it had fewer units under economic dispatch and as a result less flexibility in responding to operating conditions affecting reliability

[10] 11/13/96 FERC Order; mimeo, p. 18, at f.n. 67

[11] Remaining ancillary services include regulation and frequency, energy imbalance, operating reserve-spinning, and operating reserve-supplemental

[12] 11/13/96 order; p. 18

[13] Under Section 7.4 of the PJM tariff the ISO is required to credit to each holder of firm transmission rights (*i.e.,* a transmission customer holding firm point-to-point transmission service or a network customer) a *pro rata* share (determined on load ratio shares, as adjusted) of the revenues received under the tariff for non-firm point-to-point transmission service and firm point-to-point transmission service during the previous calendar year, if any

14 Terms and conditions of the PJM OASIS and standards of conduct are set forth in 18 C.F.R. § 27 of FERC's regulations. See Section 4 of the PJM tariff

15 The forecast pool requirement means the aggregate level of capacity resources required under the RSA as determined by the reserve sharing committee. §1.19, RSA. The forecast pool requirement is established to ensure a sufficient amount of capacity to meet the forecast load plus the reserves to provide for the unavailability of capacity resources (see definition, *infra*), load forecasting uncertainty and planned and maintenance outages. § 7.1, RSA

16 Capacity resources mean the MW of net capacity from owned or contracted for generating facilities accredited to a party under the RSA. §1.8, RSA

17 RSA, § 6.6

18 RSA, Schedule 16, §2

19 Application, 7/24/96, Vol. I; mimeo, p. 20

20 Ibid

21 ISOA, § 6.2(b)

22 Application, Vol. I; mimeo, pp. 23-24

23 ISOA, §§ 14.1 and 14.2. Removal required either a majority vote by each of the three administrative committees, or a two-thirds vote by two of the administrative committees and a one-third vote by the other administrative committee

24 Application, Vol. I; mimeo, p. 24

25 Ibid

26 Ibid. (citing Order No. 888 at p. 31,731)

27 ISOA, § 3.2

28 ISOA, § 14.4(a)

29 *Atlantic City Electric Company et al.*, 77 FERC ¶ 61,148 (1996). PECO's restructuring plan was also rejected

30 FERC found the proposed tariff, although loosely based on the *pro forma* tariff promulgated in Order No. 888, deviated from it in several significant respects:

- point-to-point transmission service is curtailed before network service, and short-term firm point-to-point service is curtailed before long-term firm point-to-point service
- point-to-point service is available only out of or across the PJM control area
- point-to-point service is not available for imports or transactions within the PJM control area
- the PJM companies would provide themselves with network and ancillary services at no charge, while others paid

- although a network customer may receive credit for its transmission facilities, to do so it must become a party to the TOA, under which it cannot create its own zone and is not relieved of the obligation to pay transmission charges (*i.e.*, it cannot receive reciprocal service without additional charge)
- a network customer is not permitted to designate as a network load a load that is located outside the PJM control area
- the PJM companies are not required to take service for wholesale trades among the pool members

[31] *Id.* at p. 57

[32] Pursuant to Section 1 of the Agreement Among the PJM Transmission Owners to Provide a Pool-wide Open Access Tariff (Interim Agreement), filed as part of the FERC submission, the "filing of a PJM tariff may contain alternative language representing differing positions of individual parties on specific issues . . ."

[33] Under Section 2 of the Interim Agreement, after December 31, 1996, "the Parties' transmission facilities shall continue to be operated as part of a single control area with free-flowing transmission ties in accordance with the PJM Interconnection Agreement. The PJM Office of the Interconnection shall initially manage the operation of the Parties' regional bulk power transmission facilities in accordance with the PJM Interconnection Agreement until any future restructuring is in place." The Interim Agreement also delegated to the OI responsibility for administering the PJM tariff (Section 3), empowered the OI to compel installation of additional transmission facilities (Section 4.1), and allocated the costs and revenues of PJM's high-voltage transmission facilities (Section 4.2)

[34] Each party in a sector was to have one vote. The votes within a sector were then to be split in direct proportion to the number of votes cast within the sector. For example, a 62 to 38 vote in one sector would result in .62 votes in favor and .38 against. Affirmative votes totaling two-thirds of the votes cast from all of the represented sectors would then be necessary to elect the board

[35] 12/31/96 Transmittal Letter, Docket OA97-000, p. 8

[36] The PJM companies and PECO had three primary areas of disagreement with respect to the PJM tariff:

- transmission rate design
- the appropriate method for calculating and recovering transmission congestion costs
- jurisdiction over transmission services to retail native load customers

[37] The transmission owners were not actually to pay the network service tariff rate but were instead to be allocated costs on a basis reflecting their cost responsibility under the PJM tariff

[38] *MidContinent Area Power Pool et al.*, 78 FERC ¶ 61,203 (1997)

[39] The Commission supported PECO's congestion pricing proposal "for interim implementation only because there are unresolved questions on how to implement the [PJM Companies'] proposal and what modifications can make it workable." Ibid; mimeo, p. 5. The Commission stated further its belief that the PJM companies' proposal "will promote more efficient trading and will be more compatible with the type of market mechanisms we are encouraging." Ibid

[40] In its letter dated April 1, 1997 transmitting the OA for filing at FERC, the PJM stated:

> "Several versions of the Operating Agreement have been widely distributed. . . .The Operating Agreement was reviewed with all stakeholders in a public meeting on March 20, 1997 and further revised at a meeting with the stakeholders on March 31, 1997
>
> "On March 31, 1997, a meeting was held among the parties to the PJM Interconnection Agreement and all other stakeholders who have begun the application process for membership. The PJM Board was elected at that meeting based on the voting procedures first set out in the PJM Interconnection Agreement, and was ratified pursuant to the substantively identical provisions in the Operating Agreement . . ."

[41] Section 18-214

[42] When PJM was converted from an unincorporated association to a limited liability company and subsequently achieved ISO authorization, the transmission owners continued to own not only their transmission lines, transformers, and other related electrical system equipment but also the PJM office complex, including the control center, service center, furniture, equipment, and computer hardware and software. PJM had no property rights in any of these assets. Neither the Commission's November 1997 order confirming PJM's ISO status nor any of the key agreements that established PJM as an ISO addressed the question of such property rights

[43] Operating Agreement (4/1/97) recital, p. 1

[44] Operating Agreement, § 3.1(a)

[45] Operating Agreement, § 4.1

[46] Operating Agreement, § 1.10. Under § 7.4 the management committee is to establish the Office of the Interconnection

[47] Operating Agreement, § 5.1

[48] Operating Agreement, § 7.1

[49] Operating Agreement, §§ 12.1 and 13

[50] Operating Agreement, § 7.2

[51] Ibid

[52] "Of the seven Board Members, four shall have expertise and experience in the areas of corporate leadership at the senior management or board of directors level, or the professional disciplines of finance or accounting, engineering or utility regulation. Of the other three Board Members, one shall have expertise and experience in the operation or concerns of transmission dependent utilities. one shall have expertise and experience in the operation or planning of the transmission systems of investor-owned utilities, and one shall have expertise and experience in the area of commercial markets and trading and associated risk management." Ibid

[53] Operating Agreement, § 7.3

[54] Operating Agreement, § 7.8

[55] Operating Agreement, § 8.1

[56] Operating Agreement, § 6.1

[57] Operating Agreement, § 7.2

[58] Operating Agreement, § 22.5

[59] Operation Agreement, Schedule 9.04

[60] Responses filed in FERC Docket Nos. OA97-261-000 and ER97-1082-000 per letter dated April 14, 1997

[61] Executive Summary of Philip G. Harris filed in at FERC on May 9. 1997. At the time of the technical conference, PJM had developed a locational pricing algorithm and data support system to implement the PJM companies' proposal. The algorithm calculated locational marginal prices for all buses in the PJM control area. PJM also implemented a new state estimator to support system requirements, created on-line dispatcher logging systems to provide immediate data availability and created data bridges to capture existing data required for real-time locational marginal price calculation. Locational marginal prices are calculated at five-minute intervals for each of the 1,601 buses in the state estimator model and for interface buses in the PJM control area. The locational marginal price for a particular bus is based upon the incremental cost to serve load at the operating limit taking into account flexible generator offer prices and the location of that bus with respect to transmission limitations. The locational marginal price calculation uses an incremental linear optimization method that is formulated at the actual operating point. The objective is to minimize costs given actual system conditions, including system constraints

[62] In Docket No. ER97-3273-000 PECO, Coalition For A Competitive Electric Market, Schuylkill Energy Resources, and NJPIRG Citizens Lobby submitted "A Plan For The Restructuring Of The PJM Interconnection." The plan proposed to restructure the PJM pool by:
- modifying the PJM governance structure to include public interest and end-use consumer representatives and implement a transition to a so-called end state vision

- requiring the Office of the Interconnection to unbundle transmission provider and energy market functions over a six-month period
- upon full separation, converting PJM into a for-profit ISO
- concurrently with such conversion, causing the ISO to assume full operational control over the transmission assets in the PJM control area

As envisaged, the ISO would have an open access tariff on file with the Commission that would phase out zonal rates over a three-year period, after which the entire PJM control area would be subject to a single, system-wide rate

[63] Specifically, each month any congestion charges collected in an hour in excess of those needed to provide a complete hedge for each holder of FTRs are used to make up any deficiencies incurred in any prior hour in the amount by which the congestion charges collected are not sufficient to provide a complete hedge. Any congestion charge revenues remaining at the end of the month after such allocation are then credited to network and firm point-to-point customers during the month. The PJM companies also contemplated tradeable FTRs. From a trading perspective, each of potentially hundreds of bus-to-bus rights would be fungible, resulting in a highly liquid secondary trading market for FTRs. In the secondary market, any market participant, including non-firm transmission customers, would be able to purchase FTRs at market prices reflecting the participants' expectations and stream of congestion cost credits associated with each FTR. No approval by the ISO would be necessary for such market trades, since the traded FTRs would be among those already determined to be simultaneously feasible. To facilitate trading, an auction process was to be developed

[64] In 2000 FERC authorized PJM to implement a two-settlement system that allows market participants to conclude transactions for next-day delivery, thereby increasing price certainty and market flexibility. See *PJM Interconnection, L.L.C.*, 91 FERC ¶ 61,148 (2000)

[65] In 1999 FERC approved detailed procedures relating to the auctioning of FTRs. See *PJM Interconnection, L.L.C.*, 87 FERC ¶ 61,054 (1999)

[66] PJM tariff, § 34.1. By abandoning the 12-month rolling average method, the demand charge calculation was deemed more responsive to changes in load responsibility and to provide greater rate certainty, especially when customers in a retail choice context may change suppliers on a monthly basis. The change in the demand charge required changes in Sections 1.16, 1.47a, 34.2 and 34.3 of the PJM tariff to eliminate provisions needed to calculate a zonal load ratio share and changes for Attachment H for each zone to add a network service rate for each zone, based on the same annual revenue requirements and zonal coincident peak loads reflected in the PJM tariff as previously in effect

[67] The forecast pool requirement provides information to the marketplace and regulators about the future capacity needs of the PJM control area as the predicate for determining the need for additional capacity resources in time for those resources to be permitted,

sited, and constructed. It also provides the basis for advance planning and commitment by the parties for capacity resources adequate to supply the operative reliability needs of the PJM control area. Finally, it supports after-the-fact capacity accounting that measures whether the parties have satisfied their commitment to provide the required capacity resources

[68] *Atlantic City Electric Co. et al.,* 77 FERC ¶ 61,148 (1996)

[69] Attachment B; mimeo, p. 1

[70] An early test of the PJM board's authority arose in connection with PJM's proposed amendment of the PJM tariff to eliminate provisions allowing the re-dispatch of generating resources for non-firm transmission service willing to pay congestion charges. See FERC Order issued July 18, 1997 in Docket No. ER97-3463-000. PECO Energy had protested in that docket that PJM lacked authority to file an amendment to the PJM tariff under Section 205 of the FPA. FERC disregarded PECO's argument, stating that, upon its filing effective March 1, 1997, the PJM tariff was subject to future modification by FERC. PJM viewed itself as a public utility under the FPA with discretion to make tariff amendment filings

[71] Attachment B; mimeo, p. 5

[72] Ibid

[73] If the PJM board were to adopt a capital budget contemplating expansion of the PJM transmission grid, the PJM board noted, the transmission owners would have an obligation to build and bear the costs of that expansion under Article 7 of the TOA

[74] Operating Agreement

[75] Comments; mimeo, p. 12

[76] *MidContinent Area Power Pool et al.,* 78 FERC ¶ 61,203 (1997)

[77] By order issued March 10, 1999 in Docket No. ER97-3729-000, FERC approved the PJM companies' request for market-based pricing authority. See *Atlantic City Electric Company et al.,* 86 FERC ¶ 61,248 (1999). See also discussion below at p. 70 *et seq*

[78] The PJM companies also committed to amend the proposal by December 31, 1997 to establish a multi-settlement system allowing market participants to commit and obtain commitments to energy prices and transmission congestion charges in advance of real-time dispatch

[79] See Joskow and Frame, *Report on Horizontal Market Power Analysis* (July 14, 1997), pp. 14-15 (hereafter, *Report*)

[80] *Report,* p. 110

[81] The *Report* did not consider two other ancillary services—1) scheduling, system control, and dispatch service and 2) reactive supply and voltage control from generation sources service—because these services were to remain cost-based rather than market-based. *Id.* at p. 114

[82] FERC did not authorize PJM to implement market-based pricing for regulation service for several years. *PJM Interconnection, L.L.C.*, 91 FERC ¶ 61,021 (2000). Under the rules approved by FERC, market participants may submit bids to supply regulation on a day-ahead basis and will be compensated on a bid basis. All market participants will submit bids via the Internet, and results of the market will be similarly communicated. The rule also provides for automatic monitoring and verification of the provision of regulation service

[83] Operating Agreement, Schedule 1, § 3.2.3

[84] *Report*, p. 120

CHAPTER FOUR

FERC Authorization

On November 25, 1997 FERC issued its order conditionally accepting PJM's open access tariff and power pool agreements and recognizing its establishment as an ISO.[1] The order is a landmark in PJM's restructuring. It confirmed PJM's successful transition from power pool administrator to ISO and vindicated the PJM companies' positions on most issues in their ongoing dispute with PECO Energy. Given FERC's rejection of the prior PJM restructuring proposal, the order evidenced the parties' ability to reshape that proposal in compliance with Order No. 888 and to do so with stakeholder concurrence.

The PJM Transmission Tariff

As proposed by the PJM companies, the PJM tariff offered pool-wide open access transmission service on a comparable basis throughout and across the PJM control area, using the facilities of the PJM companies. Both firm and non-firm transmission users were required to pay a single, non-pancaked transmission service rate based on the costs of the transmission system at the point of delivery.[2] The single-system rate was therefore not uniform but reflected instead the cost of each transmission owner's local service area. The proposed rate was designed to avoid cost shifting for a five-year transition period until adoption of a system-wide rate equalized costs for transmission serving loads in the same service area.

FERC found the PJM tariff reasonable during the transition period, since each power supplier would pay a rate no higher than that otherwise applicable if the PJM companies had offered transmission under their respective *pro forma* tariffs. FERC nonetheless required that a uniform, system-wide rate proposal be filed on or before July 1, 2002 for implementation by January 1, 2003, when the transition period was scheduled to expire.

As proponents of the PJM tariff, each of the PJM companies committed to adhere to its non-rate terms and conditions, pay congestion costs, receive congestion charge revenues, and pay scheduling and dispatch charges to recover the ISO's costs (*i.e.,* the costs of PJM's Office of the Interconnection). However, under the PJM tariff no transmission owner would be required to pay for the embedded cost of its own transmission facilities. FERC agreed that a transmission owner should not be obliged to pay itself for transmission service over its own transmission system.

Under the PJM tariff as filed, non-firm transmission customers would pay a single, non-pancaked transmission service rate, subject to discount, based on the applicable firm point-to-point rate using peak usage pricing. If a non-firm point-to-point customer elected to wheel through congestion instead of being interrupted, it would pay the higher of congestion costs or the transmitting utility's embedded cost rate. The ISO would then distribute revenues associated with non-firm point-to-point transactions to transmission owners in proportion to their relative revenue requirements.[3] Although it found this methodology acceptable, FERC required that revenues collected from non-firm transmission rates be credited directly to firm transmission customers on a monthly basis during the five-year transition period. Accordingly, if a non-firm customer pays congestion charges to wheel through congestion, congestion charge revenue credits to firm customers would be included in monthly bills.

Transmission congestion charges

The PJM companies and PECO differed markedly in their treatment of management of transmission congestion charges. After implementing PECO's uplift congestion management on an interim basis, FERC nonetheless adopted the PJM companies' locational marginal pricing (LMP) concept. FERC found that LMP "will reflect the opportunity costs of using congested transmission paths, encourage efficient use of the transmission system, and facilitate the development of competitive electricity markets."[4]

Under the LMP proposal each generator supplying energy to the bid-based energy exchange market would be paid the marginal price of generation at each location on the grid. When transmission constraints limit PJM's ability to call upon generation offered at one location to serve load at another location, PJM would dispatch higher price generation to serve that load. This would in turn cause LMPs to differ on opposite sides of constrained transmission interfaces. The differences between the LMPs would then represent congestion costs, *i.e.,* the increase in operating costs associated with dispatching generating sources out of merit order and foregone savings or profits.

Under the PJM tariff every firm point-to-point and network service would be accompanied by tradable fixed transmission rights (FTRs) for specific receipt and delivery point reservations, entitling the holder to receive rebates of congestion revenues. FTRs would be subject to sale to another transmission customer without reassigning the underlying transmission capacity reservation. For point-to-point service an FTR is the capacity reservation associated with each point of receipt and delivery. For network service an FTR is similarly related to each point of receipt and delivery, subject to the network customer's capacity reservation and not exceeding its annual peak load. To offset congestion charges, therefore, a firm transmission customer must schedule energy between its points of receipt and delivery for which it holds FTRs. Otherwise it will pay congestion charges to the extent it uses points that are constrained and receive congestion revenues to the extent other transmission customers use the points for which it holds FTRs when such points are constrained. In approving LMP, FERC dismissed numerous objections lodged by intervenors.

Complexity. Certain intervenors, including PECO, contended that LMP would be too intricate to be reliable or auditable and that, in any event, LMP was simply not justified by the historic magnitude of congestion within PJM, "a relatively insignificant amount when compared to the total PJM transmission revenue requirement of more than $850 million."[5] FERC cited testimony given at the technical conference to conclude LMP computations could be audited and independently verified. FERC also found that the relatively modest aggregate annual congestion charge indicated by the intervenors was understated because LMP would also encompass foregone savings and profits in connection with pool dispatch—costs previously included in bilateral transaction rates.

Lack of price certainty. Because actual congestion costs for any particular hour would not be determinable until after that hour had elapsed, power marketers were opposed to LMP.[6] They contended that congestion costs must be known before energy schedules are committed in order to provide a price signal and ensure economic scheduling decisions. They also argued that similar price uncertainty would not apply to transactions consummated through the power exchange since power exchange buyers can specify a maximum purchase price combining the wholesale generation price and the transmission congestion charge. The PJM companies observed that because congestion costs do not become certain until all last-hour changes in demand and generation levels are determined, congestion costs are unknowable until the dispatch hour. FERC directed PJM to file a revised congestion pricing proposal providing greater price certainty, while suggesting that price certainty could be addressed by requiring parties to commit to energy schedules earlier and by allowing market participants to specify the maximum congestion charge they are willing to pay in advance of scheduling a transaction.[7] In developing a day-ahead schedule, PJM would then schedule only those transmission customers willing to pay the applicable market-clearing congestion charge.

Computing congestion charges based on power exchange prices. While hourly power exchange (PX) prices were deemed appropriate to measure congestion costs related to PX transmission services, certain intervenors objected to using PX prices to compute congestion costs for such non-PX transmission services as bilateral power sales and urged that the appropriate price signal should take into account hourly, weekly, monthly, and seasonal transactions. FERC nonetheless accepted hourly PX energy prices as representative of the market-clearing price in the region, citing the interrelated nature of the bilateral and PX markets.[8]

Consistency with transmission expansion requirements. Power marketers and others argued that LMP would not provide appropriate price signals for long-term expansion of the transmission grid. FERC did not discern a difference between short-term transactions and long-term grid expansion. "[E]ven when participants engage primarily in short-term transactions, high levels of congestion costs will give participants an incentive to expand capacity . . ."[9] (In response to PJM's Order No. 2000 compliance filing, certain intervenors nonetheless continued to express concern that LMP does not provide sufficient economic incentive to transmission owners for transmission expansion. FERC recognized the concern by requesting changes to PJM's planning and expansion procedures.)

Prohibition against "and" pricing. Perhaps the most formidable objection to LMP was that it violated FERC's rule against "and" pricing, *i.e.,* that a customer may not be charged both an embedded cost rate and an incremental cost rate for the same service over the same facilities.[10] "And" pricing was thought to arise because firm transmission service customers that pay congestion charges would be forced to pay both embedded and incremental cost rates contrary to the rule. FERC disagreed, noting that a firm customer would pay only an embedded cost rate when it scheduled energy consistent with its firm reservation and, if it scheduled energy inconsistently with such reservation, would have requested a service relying on alternative receipt and/or delivery points, *i.e.,* a new service. Any payment of congestion charges for a new service by definition would not violate the prohibition against "and" pricing.

Initial allocation of FTRs. Power marketers also viewed the allocation of FTRs to every firm point-to-point and network service under the PJM tariff, based on specific receipt and delivery point capacity reservations, as a discriminatory give-away to transmission-owning utilities. FERC was not persuaded. It noted transmission providers are entitled to reserve sufficient capacity to meet native load requirements, *i.e.*, to serve the customers for whom the transmission grid was planned and constructed in the first instance, and that it would therefore be entirely consistent to assign transmission providers FTRs to support their existing firm uses of the system.

Allocation of FTRs based on network load versus network resources. Under the PJM companies' proposal, each network customer would receive FTRs for network resources associated with each point of receipt and delivery, although the total amount of FTRs so allocated would not exceed its annual peak load. A network customer would nonetheless have discretion to determine which network resources to use for the purpose of initial allocation of FTRs. These features engendered the objection that to the extent of their reserves, *i.e.*, network resources in excess of load, network customers would forego protection from congestion charges and that network customers' discretion in allocation would allow them to designate resources that are most likely to generate congestion revenues. FERC stated in response that FTRs are properly allocated to network customers based on network load. FERC also noted that since all existing resources are deemed network resources under the PJM tariff, network customers may properly select which of their network resources to exclude from congestion charge protection.

Allocation of congestion revenues to network customers. FERC identified a disconnect between the PJM tariff and allocation of congestion revenues. The PJM tariff assesses a transmission rate on the basis of network customers' monthly network loads, while congestion revenues are distributed in accordance with allocation of FTRs, assigned initially on the basis of firm contract reservation based on annual peak. FERC believed that this could allow network customers to receive a greater percentage of FTRs and congestion revenues than their percentage share of transmission costs. To avoid this difference, FERC mandated revision of the billing determinants for network service and FTR distribution.

Operating Agreement. The organizational linchpin of PJM as restructured was the modified Operating Agreement, which established the Office of the Interconnection within PJM as an autonomous body under an independent board of managers, to perform ISO functions, administer the

PJM tariff, operate the PX, and approve a regional transmission plan. Reconstituted as a limited liability company, PJM now embraced within its membership all market participants, including generation owners, other suppliers, transmission owners, distributors, and end-use customers functioning through a sectoral members committee. In its order FERC measured the Operating Agreement, and PJM's functions and structure thereunder, against the ISO principles enunciated in Order No. 888.

Fair and non-discriminatory governance. To mediate between independence and sectoral participation, PJM had installed the board of managers as an independent governing body, elected by the members committee but not under its control, and made the members committee a representative body with advisory powers.[11] This was a compromise arrived at after FERC's rejection of the initial governance arrangements, under which the PJM companies had retained ultimate control. In accordance with decisions reached at numerous stakeholder meetings, the members committee was intended to allow all market participants a forum for participation in PJM's affairs without compromising independence. FERC found the governance structure generally acceptable but ruled that members' termination, amendment of, or withdrawal from the Operating Agreement or other key agreements could not become effective without prior FERC approval.[12] Absent this change, members could have effectively exercised residual control, undercutting PJM's independence.

No financial interest. Under the rubric of financial interest, FERC addressed several interrelated but separate issues. It noted, in the first instance, that PJM's reconstitution as an ISO had been accomplished by a legal formality, *i.e.,* conversion of PJM Interconnection Association (an unincorporated association under Pennsylvania law) into a limited liability company. Absent any other change, this transformation would have left limited liability company transmission owner-members with a controlling financial interest in the ISO, a problem that FERC deemed rectified by the oversight of an independent PJM board and a sectoral members committee. A cognate concern was PJM's annual budget, prepared by the Office of the Interconnection but reviewed by the finance committee,[13] which was to submit the budget (and its comments) to the PJM board for approval. Given its composition and functions, however, the finance committee was viewed as having only an advisory role. Final budgetary authority resided instead with the PJM board. To avoid conflicts of interest, both the PJM board and PJM's officers and directors were subject to codes of conduct, which FERC enhanced by requiring divestiture of interests in any market participant within six months of hire or election.

Open access transmission. The PJM tariff was deemed to meet FERC's requirement for open access, non-discriminatory transmission at single, non-pancaked rates.

Short-term reliability. To assure short-term reliability, FERC noted that PJM would operate the PJM control area, manage the energy market, direct and coordinate operation of designated transmission facilities, administer the PJM tariff, and coordinate transmission expansion planning—all in accordance with MAAC and NERC guidelines. FERC was nonetheless particularly sensitive to PJM's ability to direct members' actions under emergency conditions in accordance with the Operating Agreement. FERC therefore required deletion of inconsistent qualifying language contained in the Transmission Owners Agreement "to the maximum extent reasonably practicable."[14]

Control over operation of interconnected transmission facilities. FERC expressed no doubt that PJM exercised control over operation of interconnected transmission facilities within the PJM control area. It required nonetheless that PJM maintain an up-to-date, publicly available register of controlled transmission lines and associated facilities so that transmission customers could determine where its responsibilities end and those of individual transmission owners begin. Left unaddressed were the transmission owners' retained ownership interests in information systems, intellectual property and land, buildings, fixtures, and equipment used by PJM in its operations. The transmission owners simply allowed PJM to use those assets as a transitional accommodation during PJM's restructuring.[15]

Identification and relief of system constraints. FERC found that PJM "will schedule and dispatch generation economically on the basis of least cost, security-constrained dispatch and the prices and operating characteristics offered by market sellers, continuing until sufficient generation is dispatched to serve the market energy purchase requirements of market buyers as well as PJM requirements for ancillary services. In the event of a constraint, [PJM] will re-dispatch generation out of economic dispatch in order to relieve the constraint and serve the needs of energy market buyers."[16]

Appropriate incentives for efficient management and administration. FERC limited its consideration of this principle to a requirement that procurement of services on behalf of PJM, including procurement from members, be open and competitive. The broader question—incentives for efficient management—was left unaddressed. Yet, as a not-for-profit limited liability company dependent on a skilled staff, PJM had reason to be concerned whether the management incentives it could offer would be competitive with those in the private sector.

Pricing policies for transmission and ancillary services. FERC noted that the PJM companies had proposed a two-part rate:

- a single, non-pancaked rate to recover transmission owners' revenue requirement
- a transmission congestion charge designed to reflect the cost of using a constrained transmission path

FERC accepted the proposal in principle, subject to a requirement that the pricing of ancillary services be further supported.

Dispute resolution. Given the complexity of the arrangements contemplated and the interests at stake, adoption of workable dispute resolution procedures was viewed as essential. The Operating Agreement contemplated an alternative dispute resolution committee and binding arbitration of disputes involving less than $1 million arising under the governing agreements, unlike disputes arising under the PJM tariff, which are separately governed by its dispute resolution procedures. In any case, FERC may vacate or modify an arbitral decision based on an error of law.

Power exchange

PJM's scope of operations extends well beyond administering a non-discriminatory open access tariff. For many years it has also run a pool spot energy market and dispatched generating resources to serve load in the PJM control area. PJM's proposed ISO functions continued the central dispatch provisions of its prior pooling arrangements. Members could deal with others bilaterally or make power sales through the power exchange. Historically, the PJM pool had priced economy energy halfway between the buyer's decremental cost and the seller's incremental cost (*i.e.*, a split-savings rate). By contrast, under the proposed arrangements, absent transmission constraints, the proposed market-clearing price for all generation (*i.e.*, both generating sources within the PJM control area and resources sold through the power exchange transferred from other control areas) would be based on the highest cost resources dispatched during a given hour. When constrained, however, the market-clearing price at each location would reflect the cost of resources able to reach that location (*i.e.*, the locational marginal price). In constrained areas, therefore, higher cost generators would displace lower cost generators cut off by congestion, and the market-clearing price would equal the higher resulting bid.

Next to locational marginal pricing, PJM's proposed power exchange functions generated the most intense stakeholder controversy. Intervenors mounted several arguments against the power exchange and its pricing methodology:

- All suppliers should not receive the highest cost bid price—each should instead be paid its actual bid price
- Locational marginal pricing in effect rebundles generation and transmission since the cost of transmission is based on the difference in generation costs at different nodes
- Power exchange transactions are favored over bilateral transactions because they are relieved from such PJM tariff requirements as applying separately for transmission service, paying a deposit, and submitting a separate transmission schedule
- PJM should not operate both the transmission system and the power exchange. Combining functions would present a conflict of interest since PJM would have an incentive to accommodate power exchange transactions to the disadvantage of bilateral and other non-power exchange transactions. PJM's involvement with generation markets should be limited to maintaining system reliability and mitigation of transmission constraints

FERC rejected these arguments. It found the uniform highest cost bid price reasonable as an incentive to sellers and a contribution to fixed cost recovery.[17] As to the alleged rebundling of generation and transmission, FERC noted that the price paid to power suppliers would reflect only the price of generation since transmission congestion charges collected through the power exchange would be separately determined and paid to FTR holders. With minor exceptions, FERC was unpersuaded that power exchange transactions enjoyed scheduling advantages. Finally, FERC found PJM's combined ISO-power exchange functions acceptable since PJM, as restructured, would have no financial or other incentive to favor transactions through the power exchange and would operate according to well-defined rules and procedures.

Regional transmission expansion plan

The Operating Agreement contains a protocol for regional transmission expansion planning, generally following NERC and MAAC criteria. The protocol obligates transmission owners to supply staff, data and systems to support a regional analysis and contemplates broad stakeholder participation and coordination with neighboring control areas. The protocol includes a recommendation for cost responsibility, allocated among transmission owners in accordance with the percentage of PJM load in each transmission owner's service area (as to 500 kV, 345 kV and 230 kV facilities) or to the transmission owner in whose service territory the expansion is located (as to 230 kV facilities).

FERC found the protocol reasonable since it provides for regional planning with the input of all affected parties, establishes a cost-sharing mechanism, and obligates the transmission owners to construct necessary facilities. (Subsequently, in its order provisionally granting PJM RTO status, issued July 2001, FERC found fault with certain aspects of PJM's regional transmission expansion planning process. FERC urged that the process explain how PJM will pursue infrastructure investment to make generation markets more competitive and reduce the influence of transmission owners by enhancing the access and ownership rights of third-party participants.)

Reliability Assurance Agreement

Reserve sharing to reduce the cost of installed capacity has been from its inception a principal rationale for the PJM power pool. To this end, PJM has developed procedures for:

- determining the pool-wide generation requirement to meet pool-wide loads, including reserves
- determining each member's individual obligation to contribute to the pool-wide generation requirement
- comparing each member's compliance with its obligation
- charging members for capacity deficiencies

To continue these procedures in modified form, load-serving entities, *i.e.,* utilities selling power at retail to loads within the PJM control area, became parties to the Reliability Assurance Agreement, the day-to-day administration of which was delegated to PJM as ISO.

To accommodate retail choice within the PJM control area, the period for recognizing changes in retail loads was reduced, and the combined capacity needs of the pool over the next five years were made subject to recomputation in each year, taking into account load projections, generating resource characteristics, outage rates (both forced and planned), demand side management options, and the capacity benefit margin.[18] The resulting determination is the forecast pool requirement.[19]

The PJM power pool interconnects with adjacent control areas. As a reliability measure, PJM member companies treat a fraction of transmission interface capacity at the point of interconnection as unavailable for individual transactions. That capacity (the capacity benefit margin) is instead reserved for the companies' own firm use in meeting generation reserve requirements, and the forecast pool requirement is reduced accordingly. FERC expressed concern that the capacity benefit margin would be inconsistent with its open access policies and the PJM tariff, which does not allow transmission owners to remove firm transmission capacity without following specified procedures. FERC withheld decision and called for briefs on the subject from interested parties.

Under the Reliability Assurance Agreement, each load-serving entity (LSE) within the PJM control area that intends to purchase power from the power exchange must become a party.[20] Intervenors questioned, as incompatible with emerging competitive markets, enforced cooperation among competitors with respect to such sensitive matters as capacity resource plans, planning and operation and reserve sharing.[21] FERC nonetheless endorsed the principle that LSEs that purchase from the power exchange must participate in the Reliability Assurance Agreement. Failure to do so, reasoned FERC, would allow the transmission owners' competitors to rely unfairly on their resources for reliability purposes. FERC did not similarly accept a proposed requirement that all parties to the Reliability Assurance Agreement be required to obtain network transmission service. FERC found instead that each LSE should be allowed to determine the type of service, network or point-to-point, which best meets its needs.

Transmission Owners Agreement

Under the Transmission Owners Agreement the PJM member companies transferred to PJM as ISO the responsibility for administration of the PJM tariff, operations and regional transmission planning. At the same time the PJM member companies retained certain residual rights to:

- make a Section 205 filings to seek recovery of their revenue requirement
- protect their electrical facilities from damage or injury
- build, acquire, sell, dispose, retire, merge, or transfer any of their assets
- fulfill federal, state, or local reliability requirements

FERC accepted the Transmission Owners Agreement subject to elimination of provisions allowing transmission owners to file unilaterally to make changes in rate design or terms and conditions of jurisdictional services, except for the right of each transmission owner to file unilaterally to change the revenue requirement under its individual jurisdictional rates. As to the PJM tariff, FERC stated that PJM as ISO "has the right and responsibility to participate in the development of any such revisions and to intervene in any proceedings pertaining to such filings."[22]

EHV agreements

As we have seen, the PJM companies, including PECO Energy, are parties to multilateral high voltage transmission agreements establishing rights to specific transmission services, primarily transmission of power from jointly owned generating units to their owners throughout the PJM control area. The EHV agreements establish a cost-sharing formula allocating costs according to usage. The PJM companies proposed to amend the EHV agreements to make them available on a non-discriminatory basis to all transmission customers, subject to cost support payments.

PECO proposed terminating the EHV agreements entirely, thereby subjecting all usage to the PJM tariff and eliminating support payments. FERC agreed to continuation of cost-sharing arrangements under the EHV agreements but eliminated dedicated usage provisions and made the agreements subject to the PJM tariff.

Existing bilateral agreements

To implement power pool restructuring, PJM was required to assume responsibility for administering all existing bilateral transmission agreements within its control area. In doing so, PJM was to arrange scheduling, include additional transmission obligations in its planning exercise, and integrate bilateral and PJM tariff services.

FERC directed that all bilateral agreements be revised to eliminate multiple transmission service charges. Thus, for a customer paying multiple charges to use more than one transmission system with combined rates higher than the PJM tariff rate, the combined rates were subject to reduction. Similarly, transmission owners' existing bundled power sales contracts had to be modified to eliminate the transmission component, otherwise recoverable under the PJM tariff.

Market monitoring plan

FERC's continuing oversight of undue discrimination and market power was reflected in its mandate that PJM submit a market-monitoring plan to detect design flaws or structural problems affecting operation of both pool and bilateral markets and to evaluate proposed enforcement mechanisms. Notwithstanding this mandate, market monitoring by ISOs became a controversial subject, criticized by transmission owners as an unwarranted regulatory intrusion but justified by FERC as necessary to avoid manipulation of pool rules for the benefit of transmission owners and others with economic leverage.

Conclusion

FERC's order was a watershed for PJM, validating its existence as an ISO and placing an official imprimatur on its complex transmission and power exchange methodology. FERC did not definitively resolve all issues but gave PJM the necessary predicate to be an advocate on its own behalf.

Notes

[1] *Pennsylvania-New Jersey-Maryland Interconnection et al.*, 81 FERC ¶ 61,257 (1997). The order approved the transfer of control over jurisdictional transmission facilities to PJM as ISO pursuant to Section 203 of the FPA. *Order*, mimeo p. 68

[2] Unit charges for firm transmission services are determined by dividing each transmission owner's revenue requirement by the average of its 12 monthly system peaks for a test year. The charge is then applied to contract demand for point-to-point reservations and to the monthly coincident peak load for network service

[3] The non-firm transmission service revenues subject to this distribution would be non-congestion revenues, *i.e.*, the basic charge that applies in the absence of transmission constraints. When the non-firm transmission service rate during a period of congestion is based on the higher embedded cost rate, therefore, that portion of the rate equaling the congestion charge would be distributed to holders of FTRs. If congestion charges are higher than the embedded cost rate, all of the revenues would be related to congestion charges and distributed to firm FTR holders

[4] *Order*, mimeo, pp. 37-38

[5] *Order*, mimeo, p. 42. Intervenors stated that PJM's historic congestion costs were approximately $4 million as compared to LMP's indicated congestion costs of $150 million annually. The larger amount was said to be intentionally inflated "for the purpose of transferring monies from power suppliers to RTOs." *Ibid*

[6] Transmission preschedules, generating resource availability, purchase offers, and sale offers are subject to change up to the hour of service. *Order*, mimeo, p. 44

[7] *Order*, mimeo, p. 45

[8] *Order*, mimeo, p. 46

[9] *Order*, mimeo, p. 47

[10] See *Inquiry Concerning the Commission's Pricing Policy for Transmission Services Provided by Public Utilities under the Federal Power Act, Policy Statement*, FERC Statutes and Regulations, Regulations Preamble January 1991-June 1996 [citation 1994-95]

[11] The members committee includes five sectors, as noted, each of which must have at least five members. A member can belong to only one sector and is limited to one vote within that sector. Each sector is entitled to cast one vote, which can be split into fractional components voting either for or against a measure. The sum of affirmative votes needed to pass a measure must be greater than the product of 0.0667 times the number of sectors meeting the minimum membership requirements

[12] *Order*, mimeo, p. 58. In requiring its prior approval, FERC adopted comments previously filed by the PJM board.

[13] The finance committee consists of one representative of the parties to the RAA, one representative of the parties to the TOA, two representatives of the members committee (if not also a party to the TOA), one representative of the Office of the Interconnection selected by PJM's president, and two members selected by the PJM board

[14] *Transmission Owners Agreement,* § 4.4.2. *Cf. Operating Agreement,* §§ 10.4(xx), 11.3.1

[15] See *Atlantic City Electric Company et al.,* FERC Docket No. ECOO-105-000, in which the PJM companies filed for authorization to transfer and sell the referenced assets to PJM

[16] *Order,* mimeo, p. 64

[17] FERC noted that this approach is consistent with its policy permitting sellers to earn a margin above variable costs for economy energy sales. *Commonwealth Edison Co.,* 23 FERC ¶ 61,068 at 61,232 (1979)

[18] The capacity benefit margin is the capacity available to the pool to transmission interfaces to reach neighboring control areas during emergencies

[19] *e.g.,* if the forecast pool requirement were 50,000 MW, a load-serving entity responsible for 10% of combined pool loads would be required to provide 5,000 MW of installed capacity

[20] Reliability Assurance Agreement, Article 2 and § 11.6(b), respectively. Each party to the Reliability Assurance Agreement becomes a member of the reliability committee, which has authority to revise or terminate the Reliability Assurance Agreement and approve changes to pool reliability criteria. A two-thirds majority vote in each of two voting blocks is required for action on major items. One of the voting blocks provides for one member, one vote, while the other voting block grants voting rights based on relative load, subject to a 25% cap on load-weighted votes and a requirement that three parties must dissent to block a proposal

[21] FERC required nonetheless that generation resource plans be provided directly to PJM as ISO, and not to the members. *Order,* mimeo, p. 83

[22] *Order,* mimeo, p. 84

Pricinaing

→ Bigins on PJM wholesale Mark

→ operato on Day ahead Basis

Buyers & Sellers

→ calculates hourly pricing for each
hour of next day

– Pricing Based on
total production cost

No PJM uses market based pricing

CHAPTER FIVE

PJM Market Pricing Rules

PJM members may trade electricity in the PJM wholesale energy market, which operates on a day-ahead basis. Participants submit offers to sell and bids to purchase electricity for the following day. The day-ahead market calculates hourly clearing prices for each hour of the next operating day. Prices are based on generation offers and demand bids submitted to PJM, which ranks offers and bids, from least to most expensive, based on total production dollars. The matching of bids and offers establishes a clearing price for each hour of the next day. As the demand for electricity shifts up and down throughout the day, PJM keeps supply and demand in balance by calling on or off or giving instructions to adjust generation units or transactions. The real-time market calculates hourly clearing prices based on actual system operations dispatch.

Since achieving ISO status, PJM has moved from cost-based to market-based pricing while operating the grid as an integrated, free-flowing network to which all eligible market participants have non-discriminatory access. PJM's operations as ISO rest on several critical market features.

Market-based bids

Under its market rules, any generation supplier may elect to participate in PJM's economic dispatch.[1] In so doing, a supplier may submit voluntary price and quantity bids on a day-ahead basis, specifying the prices it is willing to accept within a specified range of output. Voluntary price and quantity bids supersede PJM's previous reliance on cost-based estimates, permitting it to determine the least-cost merit order dispatch to serve all loads not met by bilateral transactions. Suppliers have equal access to all wholesale loads served, and PJM's bidding and dispatch rules apply uniformly, without regard to suppliers' ownership or affiliation.

Setting prices for energy and transmission

On the basis of voluntary price and quantity bids received, PJM also determines market-clearing prices at each location or node on the grid, *i.e.*, locational marginal prices based on the marginal cost of serving the last increment of load at each location. Market-clearing prices are paid to all suppliers participating in the economic dispatch, while differences in locational prices between the point of withdrawal and the point of injection are used to price transmission between those points and account for congestion.

Balance and reliability

In discharging its functions as ISO, PJM ensures that the grid remains in balance at all times and honors all transmission constraints to maintain reliability. After reviewing all scheduled and actual flows on the grid, PJM adjusts generation and loads as needed to maintain frequency, equilibrium between loads and resources, and meets voltage and other reliability constraints. To relieve transmission constraints, PJM is required from time to time to dispatch generation out of merit order.

This impacts market-clearing prices, which differ between locations depending on the degree of congestion and the price bids of generators and loads at each location. From an economic perspective, the difference in locational prices reflects the opportunity cost of transmission between any two points and enables PJM to set the price of transmission usage accordingly.

Fixed transmission rights

Under the PJM tariff, PJM administers a system of firm transmission reservations, allowing each load-serving entity (LSE) to reserve sufficient firm transmission for its loads. PJM provides LSEs network integration service inside the PJM control area, while all participants may reserve point-to-point service for service out of the area through the PJM control area. In connection with firm transmission reservations, users receive fixed transmission rights (FTRs) entitling the holder to compensation for congestion-related charges that arise when PJM is required to re-dispatch generators out of merit order to relieve congestion. FTRs are tradable price hedges that offset congestion-related transmission charges.

Locational marginal price

As noted, PJM operates an integrated dispatch/spot market that determines market-clearing energy prices at every node based on actual security-constrained dispatch. These prices are used to settle imbalances, price congestion for both spot and contract transactions, procure and price ancillary services, and settle point-to-point FTRs allocated and/or auctioned.

The locational marginal price (LMP) market reflects and prices essentially all congestion. A market participant does not need to trade actively in decentralized, day-ahead, or hour-ahead markets to try to adjust its contract positions to its latest projection of its real-time position.[2] This is instead accomplished automatically in PJM's real-time LMP market at market-determined, transparent prices (Fig. 5-1).

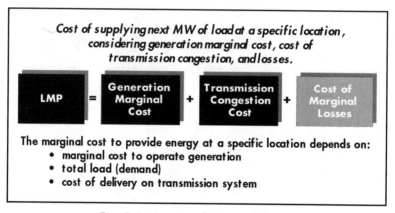

Fig. 5–1a Locational Marginal Pricing

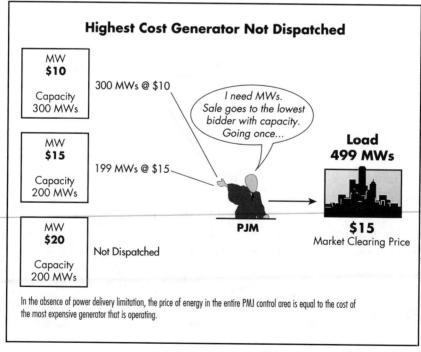

Fig. 5–1b Economic Dispatch

LMP is thus the marginal price for energy at the location where it is delivered or received. For accounting purposes, LMP is expressed in dollars per megawatt-hour ($/MWh). PJM uses LMP to calculate the price of energy at approximately 2,000 buses in the PJM control area, on a day-ahead basis for each hour of the day-ahead energy market and every five minutes during the operating day for the real-time energy market. Under an LMP regime:

- If there are no constraints on the transmission system during an hour, LMP is equal to the highest cost or bid price that PJM requests to operate during that hour—there is a single clearing price.
- When transmission congestion exists, PJM dispatches one or more generators out of economic merit order to keep transmission flows within limits. LMP then reflects the cost of re-dispatch and the cost of delivering energy to that location. When the transmission system is constrained, the congestion cost equals the difference in LMP between the source and sink, since LMPs on a constrained system will vary by location relative to the constraint. In a congested flow direction, the LMP at the origin tends to be less than the LMP at the destination. The congestion charge for delivering energy over the path is simply the difference in the LMPs multiplied by the MWs of energy being delivered. The congestion charge is inherent in the locational price. When a participant delivers energy across a constrained path, the cost of that delivery is determined by the difference in the price at the beginning and end of the path (Fig. 5-2).

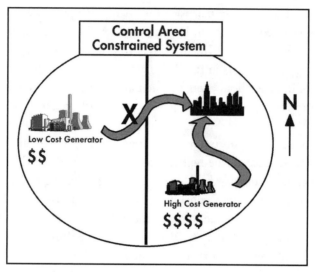

Fig. 5–2 Security Constrained Re-Dispatch Cost Example

There are two types of explicit congestion charges:[3]

- point-to-point congestion charges calculated based on the differences in LMPs between the delivery bus(es) and source bus(es)
- network service congestion charges based on differences in LMPs between aggregated load buses and generation buses

To determine actual operating conditions on the system, PJM uses a computer model of the interconnected grid, a standard industry tool called a state estimator program. The model relies on available metered inputs regarding generator input, loads, lines, transformers, and power flows. PJM obtains a state estimator solution every five minutes. The solution provides the MW output of generators and the loads at buses in the PJM control area, transmission line losses, and actual flows or loadings on constrained transmission facilities. External transactions between the PJM control area and other control areas are included in the LMP calculation based on real-time transaction schedules implemented by the PJM dispatcher.[4]

PJM determines which energy offers, submitted to the PJM interchange energy market, are following its economic dispatch instructions and uses those offers to calculate real-time prices. A resource follows economic dispatch instructions and is included in the calculation of real-time prices if one of the following criteria is met:

- the price bid is less than or equal to the dispatch rate for the segment of the PJM control area in which the resource is located
- the resource is specifically requested to operate by the PJM dispatcher

To determine whether a bid price is less than or equal to the dispatch rate, PJM compares the actual MW output of the resource in question with the market seller's offer price curve, expressed in dollars per MW of output.

To establish real-time prices, PJM determines the least costly means of serving the next increment of load at each bus based on system conditions in the most recent power flow solution produced by the state estimator program and energy offers forming the basis for the day-ahead energy market or those eligible for real-time dispatch. As explained in the PJM tariff, this calculation is made "by applying an incremental linear optimization method to minimize energy costs, given actual system conditions, a set of energy offers, and any binding transmission constraints that may exist"[5] (Fig. 5-3). The cost of serving an increment of load at each bus from each resource associated with an eligible energy offer is the sum of the price at which the market seller has offered to supply an additional increment of energy and the effect on transmission congestion costs (whether positive or negative) associated with increasing the output of the resource. The energy offer or offers that can serve an increment of load at a bus at lowest cost determine the real-time price at that bus.

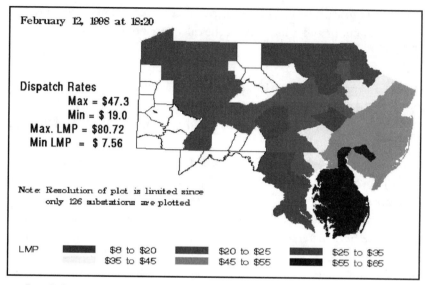

Fig. 5–3 Prototype PJM Locational Marginal Pricing Algorithm Results (LMP geographic profile for sample western interface limit)

To establish day-ahead prices for the day-ahead energy market, PJM determines LMP on the basis of least-cost, security-constrained dispatch, model flows and system conditions resulting from load specifications, offers for generation, dispatchable load, increment and decrement bids, and scheduled bilateral transactions. The calculation made on the basis of these data is the same as that used to establish real-time prices, described earlier.

LMP therefore depends on execution of sequential steps:

- Collection of system-wide data using the state estimator,[6] based on metered input and data reflecting other known system conditions processed in accordance with an underlying mathematical model
- Collection of all generator bids and current dispatch rates to analyze which generators can ramp up or down to alleviate a constraint or meet a demand. Using a locational price algorithm module (LPA),[7] PJM generates a list of "moveable" generating units, *i.e.*, units that can control flow on congested lines and thus set LMP. The price at these marginal units becomes an integral part of the LMP calculation

- Logging of current system constraints to locate areas of congestion and enable the LPA to determine where changes in locational price are necessary to meet demand
- Using the LPA to process current system bus data, moveable units, and current system constraints to generate locational prices at each bus

LMPs are used to calculate charges or credits for diverse PJM market services, including the following:

- *Spot market energy*—Calculation of charges for spot market energy purchases and credits for spot market deliveries
- *Operating reserves*—Determination whether providers of operating reserves are appropriately compensated for their costs
- *Transmission congestion*—Calculation of transmission congestion charges and determination of the value of fixed transmission rights used to calculate transmission congestion credits
- *Transmission losses*—Determination of charges for transmission losses, using weighted average LMPs
- *Emergency energy*—Calculation of charges and credits for emergency purchases and sales between the PJM control area and other control areas
- *Metering reconciliation*—Calculation of monthly error correction charges between PJM members and control areas

In general, generators are paid based on the generator bus LMP, and loads are charged based on the load bus LMP. Transmission customers or energy market buyers are charged for congestion on transactions based on the differential between source and sink LMPs.

LMP recognizes that transmission is economically equivalent to selling power at the point of receipt and buying it at the point of delivery. It allows all market participants to buy energy and transmission services at bid-based market prices. It therefore provides buyers and sellers with efficient marginal incentives in the short-term market by ensuring that all transmission and energy transactions coordinated by PJM are priced equal to marginal cost. LMP produces efficient short-run decisions for electricity consumption and transmission use while providing a market-based method to signal efficient long-run grid expansion.

In addition, LMP provides both prospective generators and loads with efficient locational incentives, ensuring use of the grid by those who place the highest value on that use and are prepared to pay the related marginal opportunity cost. By pricing congestion directly, LMP also avoids the need to sweep congestion costs over a zone into a general uplift to permit recovery, a feature of some markets that complicates determination of market-clearing prices and distorts locational prices[8] (Fig. 5-4).

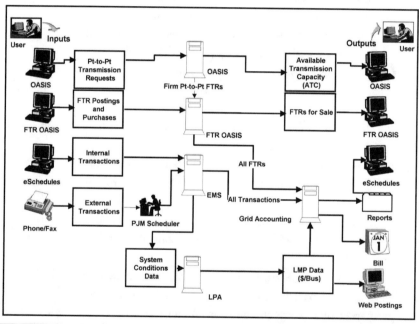

Fig. 5-4 LMP Implementation External User Interfaces

There is little doubt LMP has facilitated improved market performance within PJM. In 1999—its first full year of LMP operation—PJM scheduled, dispatched, and managed almost 50% more transactions than in the preceding year. At the same time average monthly spot market purchases increased almost 150%.

Fixed transmission rights

PJM balances the transmission system and charges for transmission use based on LMPs. When the transmission system is constrained, PJM collects more money from buyers of energy and transmission than it pays to energy sellers. This congestion rent arises because, during a period of constraint, all loads in transmission-constrained areas pay the higher market-clearing price, but generators supplying part of the flows into the transmission-constrained area are paid the lower market-clearing prices prevailing in the unconstrained area. PJM takes in more money than it pays out. Each unit of energy transferred to the constrained area causes PJM to collect, in the form of congestion payments, the difference between the LMP where energy is consumed and that where it is injected.

Transmission service customers acquiring network[9] or firm point-to-point service[10] pay the embedded cost of the system, including congestion costs for their actual use. In return, such customers also acquire fixed transmission rights (FTRs) corresponding to the points of delivery and receipt for which firm transmission service has been obtained. Each FTR entitles the holder to payment of congestion credits, if any, associated with FTR receipt and delivery points. FTRs are therefore a financial mechanism for distributing (or assigning ownership to) the congestion credits PJM collects, *i.e.*, a contract that entitles the holder to a stream of revenues (or charges) based on the reservation level and hourly energy prices across a specified transmission path.[11] An entity with firm transmission service (and corresponding FTRs) can choose to inject and withdraw power from the grid to match those FTRs, in which event the transmission charges it pays are offset by the transmission credits it receives[12] (Fig. 5-5).

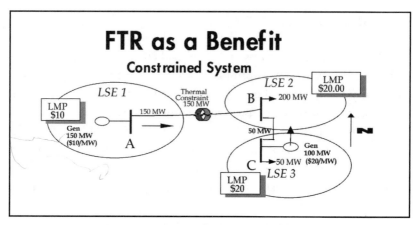

Fig. 5–5 FTR Example; Constrained System

Load serving entities (LSEs) within the PJM control area acquire network integration service to meet their peak loads and for that purpose identify capacity resources while maintaining the required reserve margin. LSEs purchasing firm network service can designate a subset of capacity resources as the origin point for FTRs from those capacity resources to the total amount of peak load for which they purchased firm network service. Each FTR is assigned from the capacity resource to the location of load in proportion to estimated peak load, subject to a simultaneous feasibility test, discussed later. Changes in network service, FTR requests received throughout the month, and FTR requests associated with monthly firm point-to-point transmission service requests are processed on a first-come first-served basis.[13]

FTRs protect firm transmission service customers from congestion costs to the extent that their energy deliveries are consistent with their firm reservations. An FTR does not entitle its holder to physical delivery of power, nor is the holder required to deliver energy in order to receive a congestion credit. If a constraint exists on the transmission system, the holder of an FTR automatically receives a credit based on the FTR MW reservation and the LMP difference between point of delivery and point of receipt.[14] The credit is paid to the holder regardless of who delivered energy or the amount delivered across the path designated in the FTR.

For network customers, as noted earlier, FTRs are designated along paths from specific generation resources to the customer's aggregated load. Although a customer may request FTRs for all or any portion of its generation resources, the total FTR designation to a zone cannot exceed the customer's total network load in that zone.[15] PJM also allocates FTRs to firm point-to-point service customers for approved service requests. The point of receipt is either a generation resource within the PJM control area or the interconnection point with the sending control area. The point of delivery is the set of load buses designated in OASIS or the point of interconnection with the receiving control area. The duration of the FTR is coextensive with the associated service request. The fact that FTRs are point-to-point need not make them illiquid because they are financial instruments with no operational effect. Sophisticated market makers can therefore hedge a portfolio of energy contracts with a correlated portfolio of FTRs.

The hourly dollar value of an FTR is based on the FTR MW reservation and the difference between LMPs at the point of delivery and the point of receipt designated in the FTR. The FTR can accordingly provide a financial benefit or a financial liability. It provides a benefit when the path designated in the FTR follows the same direction as that of the congested flow, *i.e.*, the LMP at point of delivery is greater than the LMP at the point of receipt (Fig. 5-6). It constitutes a liability when the designated path follows a direction opposite to that of the congested flow, *i.e.*, the LMP at point of receipt is greater than the LMP at the point of delivery (Fig. 5-7).

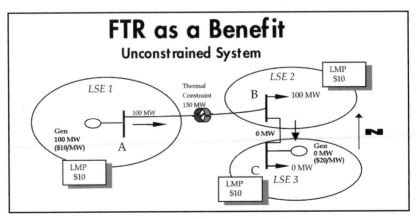

Fig. 5–6 FTR Example; Unconstrained System

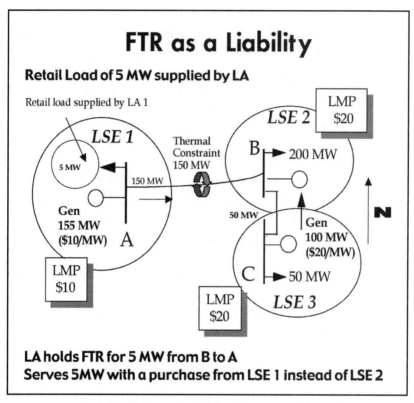

Fig. 5–7 FTR Example; Liability (Constrained System)

Before approving a network service or point-to-point FTR request, PJM conducts a simultaneous feasibility test (SFT) to ensure that the transmission system can support the subscribed set of FTRs during normal business conditions. If the FTRs can be so supported and congestion occurs, PJM will be able to collect sufficient congestion charges to cover the FTR credits. The SFT uses a DC power flow model to determine the requested firm transmission reservations and expected network topology during the period being analyzed. Inputs to the SFT model include all newly requested FTRs for the study period, all existing FTRs for the study period, transmission line outages, thermal operating limits for transmission lines, PJM reactive interface limits, and estimates of uncompensated power flow circulation through the PJM control area.

FTRs may also be acquired pursuant to an FTR auction or in the FTR secondary market[16]—a bilateral trading system that facilitates trading of existing FTRs between PJM members through a web-based bulletin board system. Since the secondary market is designed to allow bilateral trading directly between market participants, PJM's function is to track trading for accounting purposes only, and no analysis or approval of trades is performed. The FTR secondary market allows trading of existing FTRs only—no new FTR paths can be created in the secondary market.[17]

FTR auction

PJM's FTR auction procedures, initially filed at FERC in December 1997, were deemed to lack clarity and important details. In February 1999 FERC directed PJM to file new FTR auction procedures.[18] PJM subsequently submitted a compliance filing that revised the PJM tariff and the Operating Agreement and was conditionally accepted by FERC in April 1999[19] (Fig. 5-8).

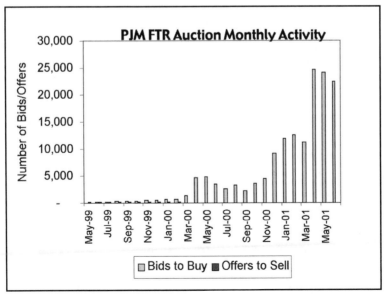

Fig. 5–8 Congestion Management

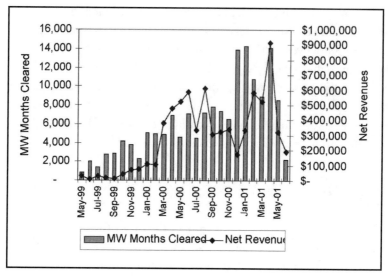

Fig. 5–8 Continued . . .

Under the new procedures, PJM conducts a monthly auction at which FTRs can be bought and sold. The FTR auction offers for sale any residual transmission entitlement available after network and long-term point-to-point transmission FTRs are awarded. PJM uses a computerized linear programming model to evaluate the bids and offers and establish FTR prices for each transmission path.[20] The auction allows market participants to sell FTRs that they are currently holding at market-clearing prices.[21] An FTR holder may also reconfigure its FTRs outside the auction process, including:

- purchase of FTRs from and sale of FTRs to other PJM members in a bilateral secondary market through eFTR, an Internet computer application
- acquisition of FTRs in connection with procurement of additional firm point-to-point service
- reconfiguration of network service FTRs[22]

The monthly auction embraces off-peak and on-peak components, each of which is separately auctioned. FTRs acquired pursuant to auction:

- have a term of one month
- are available between any single bus or combination of buses for which an LMP is calculated and posted subject to simultaneous feasibility
- may be designated from injection buses outside PJM and withdrawal locations outside PJM or buses with injections and withdrawals within PJM
- can be reconfigured, thereby enabling buyers to purchase FTRs that are different from any of the FTRs offered into the auction by sellers
- hedge the FTR holder against congestion payments to PJM when energy delivery is consistent with the FTR's definition
- do not hedge the FTR owner against payment for losses with respect to the underlying energy transaction
- are treated in the same manner as FTRs acquired in conjunction with firm transmission service for the purpose of allocating transmission congestion credits

PJM *eFTR* is an Internet application facilitating participation in PJM's auction and secondary market (Fig. 5-9). Market participants submit offers to sell or bids to purchase FTRs, which are included in the FTR auction database together with information on external grid/flow modeling, outage schedules, and facility ratings.[23] The FTR auction subsystem includes three components:

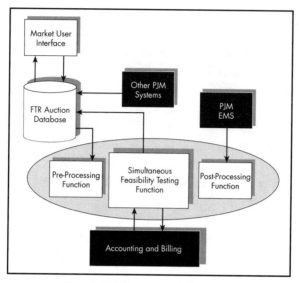

Fig. 5–9 FTR Auction Subsystems

- *Pre-processing function*—establishes a base case for evaluating quotes and prepares a set of FTRs to be tested for simultaneous feasibility
- *Simultaneous feasibility testing function*—determines and selects the highest value bid-based combination of feasible FTRs, thereby also determining the market clearing price for each FTR
- *Post-processing function*—ensures transfer of data to the auction database for posting and to accounting and billing subsystems

At the close of the bidding period each month PJM creates a base FTR power flow model that includes all outstanding FTRs approved and confirmed for any portion of the month for which the auction was conducted and that were not offered for sale in the auction. The model includes estimated uncompensated parallel flows into each interface point of the PJM control area and estimated scheduled transmission outages. PJM then determines the simultaneous feasibility of all outstanding FTRs not offered for sale in the auction and of all FTRs that could be awarded in the auction for which bids were submitted.

The winning bids are then determined from an appropriate linear programming model that selects the simultaneously feasible FTRs with the highest *net* total auction value as determined by the bids of buyers and taking into account the reservation prices of sellers. FTRs are sold at the market-clearing price for FTRs between specified pairs of receipt and deliver points. The linear programming model determines the clearing price of all FTR paths based on the bid value of the marginal FTRs, *i.e.*, those with the highest bid values that could not be awarded fully because they were not simultaneously feasible and based on the flow sensitivities of each FTR path relative to the marginal FTR path flow sensitivities on the binding transmission constraints.[24] All buyers and sellers of FTRs between the same points of receipt and delivery pay or are paid the market-clearing price, as determined at the auction.[25]

Within two business days after the close of an auction, PJM posts the winning bidders, the MW quantity, the receipt and delivery points for each FTR awarded in the auction, and the price at which each FTR was awarded.[26] All auction revenues, net of payments to sellers of FTRs in the auction, are then allocated among the regional transmission owners in proportion to their transmission revenue requirements.[27] Such revenues are taken into account in the transmission owners' costs of service that determine revenue requirements in rate cases. PJM market buyers are charged for FTR auction purchases based on the FTRs awarded (in 0.1 MW increments) and the market-clearing price, *i.e.*, the difference between prices at specified pairs of receipt and delivery points as determined by the auction. PJM market sellers are similarly credited for FTR auction sales.

Incremental FTRs

In December 1999 PJM amended the PJM tariff and the Operating Agreement to provide interconnection customers, *i.e.*, entities desiring to interconnect a generating unit to the transmission system or increase the capacity of a generating unit so interconnected, with rights to incremental FTRs. PJM had previously filed a new Part IV to the PJM tariff to establish application procedures and cost responsibility rules for the interconnection of additional generation capacity to the PJM transmission system.[28] In its order accepting that filing, FERC directed PJM to submit a proposal regarding assignment of FTRs to generation projects that pay for transmission facilities.

Following stakeholder consultation to develop an appropriate FTR proposal, PJM amended the PJM tariff to permit assignment of FTRs when a new facility or upgrade is placed in service.[29] As amended, the PJM tariff contemplates a three-round allocation process to assign incremental FTRs for specifically requested point-to-point combinations. In each round of the process, interconnection customers are permitted to request one point-to-point combination for which they desire incremental FTRs. In round one, one-third of the incremental FTRs available are assigned; in round two, two-thirds are assigned; and in round three, all available FTRs are assigned. In each round interconnection customers may change or keep the same requested point-to-point combination. In round three, however, assignments made become final and binding. When multiple interconnection customers are involved, incremental FTRs are determined based on the interconnection customers' relative cost responsibilities for the facility or the upgrade and the relative impact of the selected incremental FTRs on constrained facilities or interfaces. The incremental FTRs so assigned are effective for 30 years or the life of the facility or upgrade, whichever is less.

Incremental FTRs accord interconnection customers the economic benefits associated with funding transmission facilities or upgrades to accommodate new generation. Having borne the costs of expanding the transmission system, interconnection customers receive the incremental FTRs created by the expansion. The incremental FTRs can then be used to hedge congestion or sold in the marketplace. In the absence of incremental FTRs, entities without cost responsibility for the facilities or upgrades, i.e., free riders, would receive the incremental benefits of expansion as well as the interconnection customer, thereby reducing its incentive to build generation and transmission in the PJM control area. Incremental FTRs reinforce FERC's transmission expansion pricing policy. Since "generators will be required to pay the full cost of grid expansion," they are compelled "to consider the economic consequences of [their] siting decisions when evaluating [their] project options," a requirement that in FERC's view "should lead to more efficient siting decisions."[30]

Flowgates v. LMP

PJM's experience demonstrates that an LMP-based system with a day-ahead forward market and FTRs effectively manages transmission congestion while facilitating forward trading of energy and financial transmission entitlements.[31] Critics of LMP nonetheless contend that multiple nodal energy prices cannot have commercial significance. Alternative proposals therefore define relatively few transmission zones or flowgates with commercially significant congestion, assume that congestion in other areas of the grid will be insignificant, and address remaining congestion through an uplift charge.

Flowgate models also assume transmission congestion can be predicted and managed pursuant to long-term commercial contracts. In a zonal model it is assumed that congestion within zones will be small when compared with congestion between zones. A set of transmission rights can be defined for each of the physical zone boundaries. Since the number of zone boundaries is assumed to be small, stable and free from interaction with other zone boundaries, traders are presumed to be able to trade physical transmission rights bilaterally within a liquid and efficient market.

The foregoing assumptions have not proven valid over time. In the California market, for example, new paths with commercially significant congestion have arisen, requiring either that congestion within zones be social-ized through an uplift payment or that new zone boundaries be defined in order to manage the congestion. Neither alternative is acceptable. An uplift charge requires that all market participants pay congestion charges without regard to which transactions are contributing and provides no incentive to alleviate congestion. Defining additional zone boundaries impinges on existing transmission rights.

In the PJM market design the trading hubs and zones are based on mathematical aggregates rather than physical boundaries. As new areas of congestion develop, the aggregated LMP values reflect changing system conditions. Some existing FTRs may reduce in economic value, and new FTRs will be purchased on new constrained paths. As a result, market forces will decide how transmission reservations are valued over time. The ISO is therefore not required to intervene to manage congestion. Instead, the LMP system facilitates commerce by creating financial products that are separate from the physical market.

Between January 1, 1999 and April 30, 2000 total congestion charges within PJM were approximately $113 million, but the congestion charges attributable to 11 flowgates covering 80% of all congestion (defined using 1998 data) were only $5.4 million, leaving more than 95% to be charged by some other mechanism. Based on these results, the most highly congested paths experienced in 1998 could not be used to predict future congestion. If the remaining congestion charges were collected through uplift on every MWh of load during constrained hours, the unit uplift payment would have been $2.53 per MWh and could have been much higher depending on the method of allocation. Uplift cannot be hedged with FTRs and thus impairs liquidity in the market. In the PJM market, by contrast, traders can acquire FTRs through firm transmission service or in the FTR auction, submit transaction bids into the day-ahead market indicating the maximum congestion charges they are willing to pay, or submit hourly transactions specifying that they will curtail if congestion occurs.

Trading in capacity rights

Pursuant to the Reliability Assurance Agreement (RAA), PJM's reliability committee periodically forecasts capacity needs for the PJM control area, both to serve loads and to act as capacity reserves. In so doing, the reliability committee allocates to each member that serves load in the PJM control area a portion of the aggregate capacity requirement. If a member is deficient, it must compensate, at a fixed deficiency charge, members that have excess capacity.

To intermediate between members in deficit and in surplus, PJM has established PJM capacity credit markets as auction markets in which certain LSEs offer to sell, and other LSEs bid to buy, entitlements (credits) to use generation capacity to meet their obligations under the RAA.[32] The auction concerns only credits to generation capacity, not energy from that capacity.

The PJM capacity credit markets operate on a daily or monthly basis. In the daily auction, an LSE may offer to sell a credit for generation capacity for a particular day at a particular price (sell offer), and another LSE may offer to buy the daily capacity credit (buy bid). In the monthly market, an LSE may make a sell offer for a credit for generation capacity for a particular month during the ensuing 12 months at a particular price, and another LSE may submit a buy bid for a monthly capacity credit.[33]

After receiving all sell offers and buy bids, PJM ranks the sell offers from the lowest to the highest and ranks the buy bids from the highest to the lowest. The market-clearing price is the price at which the next (or marginal) sell offer is equal to or less than the next (or marginal) buy bid. All sellers of generation capacity in this auction receive the market-clearing price, and an LSE that does not meet its obligation under the RAA must pay a fixed deficiency charge.[34] Capacity credits thus allow market participants to manage their portfolios effectively and, like FTRs, can be traded either bilaterally or through the auction process.

Trading in capacity interconnection rights

Part IV of the PJM tariff and Schedule 6A to the Operating Agreement, accepted for filing by FERC in June 1999,[35] together establish application procedures and cost responsibility rules for the interconnection of additional generation capacity to the PJM transmission system.

To facilitate interconnection, PJM has concurrently developed and implemented capacity interconnection rights entitling a holder to deliver capacity into the grid at a particular location where the holder's generation interconnects with the PJM transmission system, although not elsewhere on the system. The rights can be freely sold or transferred, enabling merchant generators to interconnect new generation without the necessity for transmission upgrades. In this way market forces allocate scarce interconnection capacity.[36]

Market-based pricing authority

In the PJM interchange energy market (PX), PJM uses a single daily auction from which to procure both energy and ancillary services,[37] including energy imbalance, regulation and operating reserves (Fig. 5-10). Generators participating in the auction may submit a three-part bid, comprised of bids for energy (in $/MWh), start-up ($/day), and no load (in $/hour).

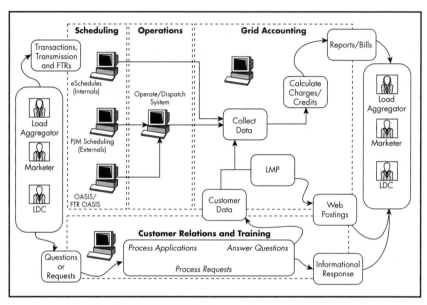

Fig. 5–10 PJM Market Pricing Process Overview

FERC has granted market-based pricing authority for energy imbalance and operating reserves services as part of its approval of market-based pricing for the PJM PX. The spot market provides the mechanism for real-time balancing, and the cost of energy imbalance bought or sold in that market is based on the LMP determined competitively. Similarly, transmission customers' cost of operating reserves is determined by the rules governing the bidding and scheduling of resources into the spot market.

Initially, however, bids were capped at cost, *i.e.,* generators bidding into the auction were required to cap their energy bids at the marginal operating cost of producing energy (generally consisting of fuel costs plus variable operation and maintenance costs). The start-up bid was capped at the costs—mostly fuel costs—incurred to bring a generator on-line. The no-load bid—also mostly fuel costs—was capped at the costs incurred to maintain a generator at minimum load after it has been started and synchronized with the system. PJM used the bids and technical plant data to determine on a day-ahead basis which generators it would schedule and, for each of those generators, the amount, if any, of energy, regulation,[38] operating reserves and ancillary services each would supply at various times during the next day. PJM also used the energy bids to determine, in real time, the energy prices for each location for each hour.

In 1997, following their application to restructure the PJM power pool, the PJM companies also filed a request that FERC lift the cost-based caps on their bids to sell energy into the PX.[39] In 1999, almost two years later, FERC issued an order approving the PJM companies' request for market-based pricing authority.[40] The order noted that, following removal of cost caps, the PJM companies would continue to provide three-part bids but would be compensated through the PX as follows:

- locational energy prices would continue to be determined based on the applicable energy bids
- regulating generators would receive the appropriate regulation capacity payment[41]
- shortfall payments would continue to be determined based on the difference between total revenue and total revenue requirement as reflected in the three-part bid

Since removal of the cost caps, however, generators' compensation no longer necessarily reflects costs.

FERC's order removing cost caps included authorization to sell through the PX at market-based rates both electric energy and certain ancillary services, including energy imbalance and operating reserves.[42] Market-based rates for regulation were deferred and became the subject of a separate application in 2000.[43] In addition, scheduling and load dispatch and reactive power voltage support services remained cost-based. FERC's order was premised on the market analysis submitted by the PJM companies, which resembled that employed in a merger context and included a definition of relevant products and geographic area leading to calculations of market shares and market concentration.[44]

FERC found that the PJM companies had "appropriately defined the relevant products and geographic markets, have presented extensive evidence on calculated market shares and market concentration measures, and have otherwise reached reasonable conclusions regarding opportunities for the exercise of market power in the energy and ancillary services markets."[45] FERC determined that, in the majority of PJM markets, concentration indices and market shares were at levels below the traditional thresholds used in market-pricing cases to determine if market power concerns exist.

As to the affected ancillary services (energy imbalance and operating reserves), FERC concluded:

- payments to providers of energy imbalance service will be tied to the PJM PX hourly spot market price for energy, a market determined to be competitive
- synchronized operating reserves are also procured in the same market as energy, *i.e.,* the only compensation available to the providers of synchronized operating reserves is that received from energy sales at the PJM PX price and the shortfall payment paid when actual revenues are less than the revenues that the synchronized generator would recover under its three-part bid, leaving as the sole avenue to exercise power the inflation of its start-up or no-load bid in order to increase its shortfall payment—a counterproductive strategy since high bids would deter PJM from dispatching a generator to produce energy[46]

Based on the foregoing analysis, FERC granted the PJM companies' request for market-based pricing authority. FERC also extended the authority granted to include other sellers, whether inside or outside the PJM control area. Such sellers may now submit market-based offers to sell energy and ancillary services into the PJM PX or pursuant to bilateral transactions used to satisfy PJM's ancillary service requirements.

Market-based pricing of regulation service

Following an extensive stakeholder process, early in 2000 PJM sought FERC authorization to amend the PJM tariff and Operating Agreement to authorize market-based pricing of regulation service, the ancillary service previously deferred as to market-based pricing. By letter order issued April 12, 2000, FERC accepted PJM's market pricing submission, conditioned upon PJM's provision of a report evaluating the efficiency and level of competition in the regulation service market after one year of experience under the new regulation service market design.

Regulation refers to the PJM control action performed to correct for load changes that may cause the power system to operate above or below 60 Hz. Regulation is accomplished "by committing on-line generation whose output is raised or lowered (predominantly through use of automatic generating control equipment) as necessary to follow the moment-by-moment changes in load."[47] As one of the six ancillary services mandated by Order No. 888, regulation must be offered to transmission customers serving load within the transmission provider's control area.[48] Under the PJM tariff each LSE within the PJM control area is assigned a share of the hourly regulation requirement based upon its share of the hourly load.[49] An LSE can satisfy its regulation obligation by:

- self-scheduling its own generation
- bilateral purchases of regulation
- purchases of regulation through the PJM regulation market[50]

Under the prior market design there was no explicit price for sales of regulation service to the PJM power exchange. Instead, generators that provided regulation service in PJM received a payment for actual energy provided plus a regulation capacity payment based on a formula intended to reflect the opportunity costs of being available for regulation service rather than energy supply. The formula contained several variables, including the amount of excess regulation capacity available, the applicable LMP at the generator's bus, and an average cost of energy for the class of regulating unit involved.[51]

To price regulation service sales made through the PJM power exchange, market participants providing regulation are paid in response to market-based offers.[52] On a day-ahead basis, market participants submit regulation offers, not to exceed $100/MWh. PJM evaluates the submitted offers and selects regulation units on a least-cost basis considering the regulation offer price, estimated opportunity costs for the units that propose to provide regulation, and PJM's obligation to minimize the total costs of energy, operating reserves, regulation, and other ancillary services. A regulation market-clearing price is established for each hour that equals the largest sum (from among selected units) of a resource's regulation offer and estimated opportunity costs.

In real-time operations, with one exception, PJM pays the market-clearing price to all units providing regulation. If a unit's actual opportunity costs in the hour—when added to the unit's regulation offer—exceed the market-clearing price, the unit receives the greater amount of its unit-specific offer and opportunity costs. In this way a generator does not suffer economically if selected to provide regulation rather than participating in the energy market when actual energy market prices vary from day-ahead predictions. PJM obtains regulation from LSEs, or other qualified suppliers of regulation offering regulation to PJM, in order to meet the pool regulation requirement after netting out the level of regulation supplied pursuant to bilateral contracts or self-scheduling.

Market participants purchasing regulation service from the market pay the market-clearing price for regulation service and share proportionally in any amounts above the market-clearing price paid to individual generators as described above.[53]

Two-settlement system

The two-settlement system allows PJM market participants the option of trading in a forward market for electric energy and embraces both a day-ahead and a balancing market.

In the day-ahead market hourly clearing prices are calculated for each hour of the next operating day based on generation offers, demand bids, and transaction schedules that are submitted into the system. The day-ahead market enables participants to purchase and sell energy at binding day-ahead prices. It also allows transmission customers to schedule bilateral transactions at binding day-ahead congestion charges based on the LMP differences between the transaction source and sink (Fig 5-11).

The Day-Ahead Market

The Day-Ahead Market is a forward market in which hourly Locational Marginal Pricing (LMP) values are calculated for each hour of the next operating day based on generation offers, demand bids and bilateral transaction schedules submitted by participants.

The Day-Ahead Market provides financial incentives for generators, retailers and transmission customers to submit day-ahead schedules that match their actual expectations for the operating day, and it provides the opportunity to obtain increased price security.

The Day-Ahead schedule is developed using least-cost, security-constrained unit commitment and security-constrained economic dispatch programs. Day-Ahead scheduling incorporates PJM reliability requirements and reserve obligations into the analysis. The resulting hourly schedules and Locational Marginal Prices (LMPs) represent binding financial commitments to the market participants.

Day-Ahead Settlement is based on the day-ahead hourly LMP values. For each hour of the day-ahead schedule:

- Each scheduled demand participant pays its LMP for the hour
- Each scheduled generator is paid its LMP for the hour
- Scheduled transmission customers pay congestion charges based on LMP differences between source and sink, and
- Fixed transmission rights holders receive congestion credits based on hourly day-ahead LMP values

---

Fig. 5–11 Two Settlement System: The Day-Ahead Market

The balancing market, on the other hand, is the real-time energy market in which hourly clearing prices are determined by actual system operating conditions as described by the PJM state estimator (Fig. 5-12).

The Balancing Market

The Balancing Market is based on real-time operations. Balancing LMP values are calculated at five-minute intervals based on actual system operating conditions as described by the PJM state estimator.

The Balancing Market provides financial incentives for generators to follow the real-time economic dispatch instructions that are issued by PJM. In the Balancing Market:

- Actual demand is met by security-constrained economic dispatch
- Capacity resources that are not selected in the day-ahead market can bid into the real-time market or then can self-schedule
- Non-capacity resources can submit bids into the real-time market

---

Fig. 5–12 Two Settlement System: The Balancing Market

Separate accounting settlements are performed for each market. The day-ahead settlement is based on scheduled hourly quantities and the day-ahead hourly prices. The balancing settlement is based on actual hourly quantity deviations from the day-ahead scheduled quantities and real time prices.[54] Both day-ahead and real-time price calculations are predicated on LMP[55] (Fig. 5-13).

Separate accounting settlements are performed for each market. The Day-Ahead Market Settlement is based on scheduled hourly quantities and on day-ahead hourly prices.

The Balancing Market Settlement is based on actual hourly quantity deviations from day-ahead scheduled hourly quantities and on real-time prices integrated over the hour.

The day-ahead price calculations and the balancing (real-time) price calculations are based on the concept of Locational Marginal Pricing.

Fixed Transmission Rights (FTRs) apply only to the Day-Ahead Market and are settled at the day-ahead LMP values.

Fig. 5–13 Two Settlement System

PJM's implementation of the two-settlement system followed a circuitous path.[56] On December 31, 1997 the PJM companies filed a proposed amendment to Schedule 1 of the Operating Agreement to establish a multi-settlement system allowing transmission customers to fix transmission costs ahead of the actual transmission transaction. By order issued February 11, 1999[57] FERC rejected the filing and directed the PJM companies to file new multi-settlement procedures within 18 months. Following an extensive stakeholder process, PJM's two-settlement system was developed in response to FERC's concern for "the lack of price certainty transmission customers face when they reserve transmission service."[58]

To create more price certainty the day-ahead market allows participants to purchase and sell energy at binding day-ahead prices. It further permits customers to schedule bilateral transactions at binding day-ahead congestion charges based on the differences in the LMP between a transaction's source and sink locations. In the day-ahead market LSEs submit hourly demand schedules, including any price-sensitive demand bids, for the amount of demand they wish to lock in at day-ahead prices. Generators designated as capacity resources[59] must submit an offer schedule into the day-ahead market unless they are self-scheduled or unavailable due to outage. Non-capacity resources may make offers into the day-ahead market but are not required to do so. Transmission customers may submit fixed or dispatchable bilateral transaction schedules into the day-ahead market and may specify the maximum amount of congestion charges they are willing to pay between the transaction source and sink if congestion occurs in the day-ahead schedule.

The two-settlement system employs several types of bidding mechanisms in the day-ahead market—price-sensitive demand bids, decrement and increment bids, and "up-to" congestion charge bids:

- *Price sensitive demand bids* are made by entities, such as LSEs, with actual physical demand, and enable a customer to place a bid to purchase a specified quantity of energy at a certain location if the day-ahead price is at or below a specified level.
- *Decrement bids* allow a marketer or transmission customer without physical demand to place a bid to purchase a specified quantity of energy at a certain location if the day-ahead price is at or below a specified level.
- *Increment bids* allow a market participant to offer to sell a specified quantity of energy at a certain location if the day-ahead price is at or above a certain price. The day-ahead market allows all market participants to use increment and decrement bidding as financial hedging tools to provide additional price certainty.

- *"Up-to" congestion bids* permit transmission customers to specify how much they are willing to pay for congestion by bidding a specified maximum amount for congestion between the transaction source and sink, *i.e.*, if the congestion charges are less than the amount specified in the bid, the transaction will be included in the day-ahead schedule. "Up-to" bids protect transmission customers from paying uncertain congestion charges by assuring they will pay no more than the amount set forth in their bids.

All spot purchases and sales in the day-ahead market are settled at the day-ahead prices, based on the bids, offers, and schedules reflecting least-cost, security-constrained unit commitment and dispatch for each hour of the next opening day. Day-ahead settlement is based on scheduled hourly quantities and day-ahead hourly prices. For each hour of the day-ahead schedule:

- each scheduled demand participant pays its LMP for the hour
- each scheduled generator is paid its LMP for the hour
- scheduled transmission customers pay congestion charges based on LMP differences between source and sink
- FTR holders receive congestion credits based on hourly day-ahead LMP values

The day-ahead scheduling process also incorporates PJM reliability requirements and reserve obligations. The resulting hourly schedules and LMPs constitute binding financial commitments to market participants.[60]

The day-ahead market thus provides financial incentives for generators, retailers, and transmission customers to submit day-ahead schedules that match their actual expectations for the operating day. It also provides the opportunity to obtain increased price certainty.

The balancing market provides financial incentives for generators to follow real-time economic dispatch instructions issued by PJM. In the balancing market:

- actual demand is met by security-constrained economic dispatch
- capacity resources that are not selected in the day-ahead market can bid into the real-time market or can self-schedule

- non-capacity resources can submit bids into the real-time market
- transmission customers can submit schedules into the real-time market

Generators that are capacity resources must participate in the balancing market or may self-schedule. If an available capacity resource is not selected in the day-ahead scheduling because its offer price is higher than that of other generators, it may alter its bid for use in the balancing market. Otherwise its original bid in the day-ahead market remains in effect. Balancing prices are calculated based on actual system operating conditions as described in the PJM state estimator. LSEs pay balancing prices (real-time LMP) for any demand that exceeds their day-ahead scheduled amounts but receive revenue for demand deviations below such amounts. Similarly, generators are paid balancing prices for any generation that exceeds their day-ahead scheduled amounts and pay for any generation shortfall below such amounts. Transmission customers pay congestion charges or receive congestion credits for bilateral transaction quantity deviations from day-ahead schedules.

All spot purchases and sales in the balancing market are settled at the balancing prices. The balancing market settlement is based on actual hourly quantity deviations from day-ahead scheduled hourly quantities and on real-time prices integrated over the hour. Balancing price calculations are based on LMPs (Table 5-1).

A Generator's day-ahead MW may be more than actual MW, as illustrated in the following tables:

1. LSE with Day-Ahead Demand Less Than Actual Demand

Day-Ahead Market	Balancing Market
Scheduled Demand = 100 MW	Actual Demand = 105 MW
Day-Ahead LMP = $20.00	Real-time LMP = $23.00
Payment = 100 * 20.00 = $2,000.00	Payment = (105 – 100) * 23.00 = $115.00

2. LSE with Day-Ahead Demand Greater Than Actual Demand

Day-Ahead Market	Balancing Market
Scheduled Demand = 100 MW	Actual Demand = 95 MW
Day-Ahead LMP = $20.00	Real-time LMP = $23.00
Payment = 100 * 20.00 = $2,000.00	Payment = (95 – 100) * 23.00 = $115.00 credit

3. Generator with Day-Ahead MW Less Than Actual MW

Day-Ahead Market	Balancing Market
Scheduled Demand = 200 MW	Actual Demand = 205 MW
Day-Ahead LMP = $20.00	Real-time LMP = $22.00
Revenue = 200 * 20.00 = $4,000.00	Revenue = (205 – 200) * 22.00 = $110.00

4. Generator with Day-Ahead MW Greater Than Actual MW

Day-Ahead Market	Balancing Market
Scheduled Demand = 200 MW	Actual Demand = 100 MW
Day-Ahead LMP = $20.00	Real-time LMP = $22.00
Revenue = 200 * 20.00 = $4,000.00	Revenue = (100 – 200) * 22.00 = ($2,200.00 payment)

Table 5–1 Two Settlement System

The two-settlement system therefore provides market participants with the option to lock in day-ahead scheduled quantities at day-ahead prices, a financial incentive for resources and demand to submit day-ahead schedules that match their actual schedules, a financial incentive for generation to follow real-time dispatch, and a means whereby resources, demand, and transactions can achieve greater price certainty. To implement the two-settlement market, PJM provides the two-settlement user interface, a web-based interface containing all the inputs and market reports necessary for trading, accessible by means of a standard format (the XML file format) for the transfer of business-related data.

Notes

[1] The following description draws upon Hogan, *Report on PJM Market Structure and Pricing Rules*, dated November 18, 1996, at pp. 2-5, filed by the PJM companies in FERC Docket Nos. ER96-2516-000 and ER96-2668-000. For further detail see Attachment K (Transmission Congestion Charges and Credits) to the *PJM tariff*

[2] Initially only PJM members could participate in the hourly market. In 1998 PJM modified its Operating Agreement, which as revised gives access to the hourly market to all market participants, including those who do not serve load within PJM. This revision gives all market participants the opportunity to schedule deliveries or receipts of spot market energy on an hour-ahead basis. See *PJM Interconnection, L.L.C.*, 84 FERC ¶ 61,224 at 62,079 (1998)

[3] PJM also determines congestion charges implicitly paid in the PJM spot market. Because LMPs reflect the increased cost of congestion, they vary depending on location. The amount PJM collects from spot market energy payments at different load LMPs will not equal the amount given out as spot market credits at various generator LMPs. The difference in the amount of payments collected and the amount of credits paid is implicit congestion. This difference is added to the total of all individual congestion charges to create the PJM control area congestion charge

[4] See *PJM tariff*, Attachment to Appendix K, Section 2.3, Revised Sheet No. 106

[5] See *PJM tariff*, Appendix to Attachment K, Section 2.5(a), p. 167

[6] The PJM state estimator is a standard power system operations tool that is designed to provide a complete and consistent model of the conditions that currently exist on the PJM power system based upon metered input and an underlying mathematical model. The purpose of the state estimator is to provide a complete and consistent solution for both the observable and unobservable portions of the electrical network

[7] The LPA contingency processor in contract curtailments mode provides a list of transmission contracts with their effect on the transmission constraint, expressed as a flow percentage, and in re-dispatch mode provides several lists of generation re-dispatch options, sorted by their dollar per MW effect on transmission constraint. Transmission constraints may involve actual thermal limit, contingency thermal limit, interface flow limit, local voltage limit, and stability limit. Responsive actions include system reconfiguration, contract curtailment and re-dispatch

[8] Hogan, *op. cit.*, pp. 45-46

[9] On an annual basis, network service customers are allocated FTRs up to their annual peak load. These FTRs are designated along paths from specific capacity resources to aggregate forecast annual peak load. The network service customer may request FTRs

from any of its designated capacity resources to its aggregated load. Network service customers may have load across multiple transmission zones. FTRs are defined separately in respect of each zone. The total MW value of all concurrent FTRs for a given network capacity resource may not exceed the summer installed capacity rating of the resource, and the total MW value of a customer's FTRs for a given network capacity resource may not exceed the customer's ownership of capacity at the resource. If capacity associated with FTRs is sold, the seller must relinquish the associated FTRs. Once the annual set of network service FTRs is established during the open enrollment period, the configuration of network service FTRs for each transmission customer is approved for the duration of the current planning period (June 1-May 31) but can be changed as often as daily by submitting a change request via the *e*Capacity system, an internet application that can be accessed through the PJM website. If approved, such requests are assumed to be valid for the remainder of the planning year. *FTR Business Rules*, pp. 6-7

In June 2001 PJM implemented a change in the method by which it allocates FTRs to network transmission customers. Under prior procedures, network customers were entitled to FTRs in an amount equal to their peak load responsibility. However, the quantity of FTRs held by most network customers presently falls well below this level. Most network customers were therefore not required to surrender any FTRs when they lost load. This limited the availability of network service FTRs to customers that changed suppliers. To address that situation, PJM implemented a new annual procedure whereby all network FTRs that are requested in an open enrollment period are allocated, using a simultaneous feasibility analysis, in proportion to requested MW amounts and in inverse proportion to the impact of the request on transmission constraints, thus eliminating the "grandfathering" inherent in the prior allocation procedure. See Answer of PJM Interconnection, L.L.C., in *Old Dominion Electric Cooperative v. PJM Interconnection L.L.C. and Connectiv,* Docket No. EL00-96-00

[10] Firm point-to-point transmission users can request FTRs for their associated firm reservations. The path of the FTR is equivalent to the path of the firm reservation from source to sink. The source is either the generation source within PJM or the interconnection point from the sending control area. The sink is the set of load busses designated in OASIS or the point of interconnection with the receiving control area. The path for each point-to-point service FTR is defined from the OASIS point of receipt to the OASIS point of delivery for which the customer has firm point-to-point transmission service. For firm point-to-point service out of the PJM control area, the point of receipt is the generation resource within the PJM control area, and the point of delivery is the interface with the receiving control area. For firm point-to-point service through the PJM control area, the points of receipt and delivery are the interfaces with the sending and receiving control areas respectively. The duration of a firm point-to-point FTR is the same as the associated firm transmission service. *FTR Business Rules*, p. 9

[11] An FTR financially binds the owner to the transmission congestion activity on that path. The path is defined by the transmission reservation as the point where the power is scheduled to be injected into the PJM grid (source) to the point where it is scheduled to be withdrawn (sink). Once determined, the FTR is in effect for the predefined period whether or not energy is actually delivered. See *PJM Interconnection, L.L.C. Fixed Transmission Rights Business Rules* filed as Exhibit A to PJM's compliance filing dated March 2, 1999 in FERC Docket No. ER99-2028-000 (hereafter, *FTR Business Rules*), p. 1

[12] Hogan, pp. 51-53

[13] Under wholesale competition an LSE can change the designation of its capacity resources and loads throughout the capability period, but the amount of change in loads and resources may be greater under retail competition as loads switch between suppliers from month to month. Following the initial designation of capacity resources and loads in the annual planning process, each LSE will acquire network firm service to meet its projected annual peak load and designate capacity resources sufficient to meet its annual peak load while maintaining the specified reserve margin. LSEs whose customers change from month to month because of retail competition may have a peak load responsibility that changes on a daily basis. Such LSEs will identify the daily revised peak loads, purchase different amounts of network firm service, and identify a higher or lower number of capacity resources. The cap on the number of FTRs that such an LSE could designate in conjunction with network transmission service would therefore change on a daily basis consistent with the changes in the LSE's peak load responsibility. *FTR Business Rules*, p. 4

[14] An FTR's economic value is based on the MW quantity multiplied by the difference between the LMPs of the source and sink points. Such LMP differences reflect the opportunity cost of the transmission path. *FTR Business Rules,* p. 1

[15] Network customers make FTR requests and modifications through an Internet computer application called eCapacity

[16] The following description appears in *FTR Business Rules*, pp.1-2

[17] Reconfiguration of FTRs' source and sink points is not permitted in the secondary market. However, a customer may in effect reconfigure its FTR position as follows: If the customer owns an FTR from Point A to Point B and wishes to change its position from Point A to Point C, it can purchase an existing FTR from Point B to Point C on the secondary market. The combination of the FTRs from Point A to Point B and from Point B to Point C results in the desired composite FTR position from Point A to Point C

[18] *Atlantic City Electric Company et al.,* 86 FERC ¶ 61,147 (1999). See generally *FTR Auction, Report to the Federal Energy Regulatory Commission,* Market Monitoring Unit, PJM Interconnection, L.L.C. (August 1, 2000)

[19] *PJM Interconnection, L.L.C.,* 87 FERC ¶ 61,054 (1999). See Section 7 of the *PJM tariff* and Section 7 of the Operating Agreement, respectively

[20] PJM uses linear programming to choose the amount of FTRs on various paths to be allocated to various bidders. The objective is to maximize total net auction value to bidders based on the bids submitted by participants. The constraints and restrictions include physical capacity limits of the various transmission lines

[21] Section 7.3.6(c) of the PJM tariff provides "Fixed Transmission Rights shall be sold at the market-clearing price for Fixed Transmission Rights between specified pairs of receipt and delivery points, as determined by the bid value of the marginal Fixed Transmission Right that could not be awarded because it would not be simultaneously feasible. The linear programming model shall determine the clearing prices of all Fixed Transmission Rights paths based on the bid value of the marginal Fixed Transmission Rights, which are those Fixed Transmission Rights with the highest bid values that could not be awarded fully because they were not simultaneously feasible, and based on the flow sensitivities of each Fixed Transmission Rights path relative to the marginal Fixed Transmission Rights paths flow sensitivities on the binding transmission constraints."

[22] Under the PJM tariff (Sections 28.1 and 30.7) network service customers are allowed to reconfigure their FTRs only between their network resources and their load. This requirement is intended to assure that the physical requirements of network service are satisfied. By contrast, in the auction, PJM reconfigures for periods of one month all FTRs offered for sale by FTR holders, including network service customers, without regard to maintaining a link between specific resources and loads

[23] An offer to sell a specified MW quantity of FTRs constitutes an offer to sell that quantity or less and may not specify a minimum quantity. Bids to purchase likewise constitute an offer to by a specified quantity or less and may not specify a minimum. *PJM tariff,* § 7.3.5

[24] *PJM tariff,* § 7.3.6

[25] *PJM tariff,* § 7.3.8

[26] *PJM tariff,* § 7.37

[27] *PJM tariff,* § 7.39

[28] See *PJM Interconnection, L.L.C.,* 87 FERC ¶ 61,299 (1999)

[29] See *PJM tariff,* §§ 1.14, 36.6.3, 42, and Attachment K. Section 42.5 of the PJM tariff provides that an interconnection customer will not receive incremental FTRs with respect to transmission investment that is included in the rate base of a public utility and on which a regulated return is earned. In that event, FTRs created by the new facility will instead be available in the FTR auction

[30] *PJM Interconnection, L.L.C.,* 87 FERC ¶ 61,299 at 62,204 (1999)

[31] The discussion in this section is based on a PJM white paper dated September 15, 2000, *Can Flowgates Really Work?,* authored by Andrew L. Ott

[32] *PJM Interconnection, L.L.C.,* 86 FERC ¶ 61,017 (1999); mimeo, p. 2. An LSE is defined as any entity that sells power at retail to end use loads within the PJM control area. See *Operating Agreement* § 1.18. An entity may also participate in the PJM capacity credit markets if it has a contractual obligation to sell capacity for use in the PJM control area

[33] For the period between January 1 and May 31, 1999, to support retail competition in Pennsylvania, participants with excess credits were required to sell them, and participants with deficient credits were required to buy them through the daily PJM capacity credit markets

[34] See generally Schedule 11 to Operating Agreement, §§ 3.1, 7.4, 6.5, 6.6, and 5.6

[35] *PJM Interconnection, L.L.C.,* 87 FERC 61,299 (June 17, 1999)

[36] Prior to filing its new generation interconnection procedures with FERC, PJM had more than 70 pending requests for interconnection and subsequently has received numerous additional requests, demonstrating that an independent ISO can promote the siting of generation in its control area and further the development of competitive markets. See *Comments of PJM Interconnection, L.L.C.,* dated August 16, 1999, Docket No. RM99-2-000; mimeo, pp. 30-31

[37] The PJM PX differs from the California power exchange, which is separate from the California ISO. In California, sellers submit energy bids into the power exchange; and the ISO purchases ancillary services (regulation, spinning, and non-spinning reserves) in separate auctions that proceed and clear on a sequential basis. *AES Redondo Beach, L.L.C. et al.,* 85 FERC ¶ 61,123 (1998); *Pacific Gas and Electric Company et al.,* 81 FERC ¶ 61,112 (1997). See also *Atlantic City Electric Company et al.,* 86 FERC ¶ 61,248 (1999); mimeo, f.n. 17

[38] Regulation service provides "for the continuous balancing of resources (generation and interchange) with load and for maintaining scheduled Interconnection frequency at sixty cycles per second." *PJM tariff* Schedule 3. Stated differently, regulation refers to the PJM control action that is performed to correct for load changes that may cause the power system to operate above or below 60 Hz

[39] The PJM PX bidding rules allow generators to submit different energy bids for each hour and a new set of bids daily. However, a generator's start-up and no-load bids, once submitted, remain in effect for six months at a time

[40] *Atlantic City Electric Company et al.,* 86 FERC ¶ 61,248 (1999)

[41] Neither the PJM tariff nor the Operating Agreement uses the term "regulation capacity payment" to describe the way in which the generators that PJM schedules for regulation service are compensated. That compensation is based on a detailed formula that contains several variables including, but not limited to, the amount of excess regulation capacity that is available, the applicable LMP and an average cost of energy for the class of regulating unit involved. *PJM tariff* Schedule 3

[42] The PJM companies noted that the price of energy imbalance service is settled using a percentage of the price of energy in the PJM hourly spot market, where the exercise of

market power is unlikely. Accordingly, the exercise of market power in the energy imbalance service market was also deemed unlikely. As for operating reserves, the PJM companies argued that generators would find it difficult to exercise market power in the provision of spinning reserves because the generators would in doing so have to sacrifice potential profits in the much larger energy market. In addition, PJM rules only allow generators to change their start-up and no load bids twice a year, thereby limiting opportunities for generators to exercise market power with respect to those ancillary services. Finally, energy prices received by quick start units used to provide or support the provision of spinning reserves are calculated so that energy payments made are not used in determining LMP at the time a quick start unit is dispatched out-of-merit order. The PJM companies also proposed that the bids of generators called to operate for reliability purposes (*i.e.*, must run units) be capped at:

- the average LMP during a recent comparable period when the generator was in the merit-order dispatch
- a level based on costs plus a 10% adder
- an amount negotiated in advance between the ISO and the generator. Several inter-venors at FERC argued that price caps should apply, if at all, only to the PJM companies, not new market entrants, and that price caps would stifle useful price signals

Atlantic City Electric Company et al., 86 *FERC* ¶ 61,248 (1999); mimeo, pp. 13-16, 19-20

[43] See *Application* filed in FERC Docket No. ER00-1630-000 on February 15, 2000

[44] *Atlantic City Electric Company et al.,* 86 FERC ¶ 61,248 (1999)

[45] Ibid; mimeo, pp. 23-24

[46] Ibid; mimeo, pp. 25-26. FERC distinguished between operating reserves synchronized to the grid and those that are not. As to the latter, no market analysis is required because PJM pays no separate compensation to unsynchronized generators. Thus operating reserves not synchronized to the grid are not eligible to receive the shortfall payments associated with 3-part bids, and the operators of such operating reserves have no opportunity to exercise market power. (Ibid)

[47] *PJM tariff* Schedule 3. The PJM manuals further define "regulation" as "[t]he capability of a specific generating unit with appropriate telecommunications, control and response capability to increase or decrease its output in response to a regulating control signal. The Capacity Resources assigned to meet the PJM Regulation Requirement must be capable of responding to the AR (Area Regulation) signal within five minutes and must increase or decrease their outputs at the Ramping Capability rates that are specified in the Offer Data that is submitted to PJM . . . [T]he Regulation capability of an individual generator is the difference between its current operating level and the level that it could ramp to, either up or down, within five minutes."

Within PJM, there are 516 generating units, of which 107 units are qualified to provide regulation service. Out of more than 56,000 MW of installed generation capacity in the

PJM control area, there are 2,392 MW of regulation capability. PJM establishes separate regulation requirements for off-peak and on-peak hours. The on-peak regulation requirement is equal to 1.1% of the forecast on-peak load for the forecast period and is equivalent to approximately 575 MW. The off-peak requirement is equal to 1.1% of the lowest forecast demand for the forecast period and is equivalent to approximately 220 MW of regulation capability

[48] FERC designated six ancillary services in Order No. 888, including:

- scheduling, system control, and dispatch service
- reactive supply and voltage control from generation sources service
- regulation and frequency response service
- energy imbalance service
- operating reserve-spinning reserve service
- operating reserve-supplemental service

Promoting Wholesale Competition through Open-Access Non-Discriminatory Transmission Services by Public Utilities, Order No. 888, 1991-96 FERC Stats. & Regs., Regs. Preambles ¶ 31,036, at 31,703 (1996), *order on reh'g*, Order No. 8888-A, III FERC Stats. & Regs., Regs. Preambles ¶ 31,048, at 30,226 (1997)

[49] *PJM tariff* Schedule 3 § (e)

[50] *PJM tariff* Schedule 3 § (f)

[51] *Atlantic City Electric Co.*, 86 FERC ¶ 61,248 at 61,894 & n. 18 (1999). On a quarterly basis PJM determined the operating cost of regulating units in three cost classifications representing base, marginal, and peaking hours. After units were assigned to a class, an average operating cost for each class was calculated by first determining the cost for each unit by multiplying the amount of certified regulation capability in MW by the average energy offer in $/MWh of the unit. The costs for all units in the class were then summed and divided by the total regulating MW in that class in order to determine the MW-weighted average cost for that class

[52] Although a generator providing regulation service will receive its LMP for all energy output, in order to provide regulation the generator often will have to set its output above or below its economic dispatch level so that it is capable of increasing or decreasing output in response to the regulating control signal. The difference in energy revenues (or costs) resulting from this change in output constitutes the generator's opportunity costs. See Section 3.2.2(e) of *Appendix to Attachment K of the PJM tariff*, which specifies how PJM determines payments to generators providing regulation service. The unit-specific opportunity cost of a resource is equal to the product of:

- the deviation of the resource's output level from the level at which it would have been dispatched in economic merit order

- the absolute value of the difference between the LMP at the bus for the resource and the offer price for energy from the resource at the PJM PX (at the MW level of the regulation set point for the resource)

If the actual opportunity cost when added to the unit's regulation offer is higher than the market-clearing price, the higher amount is paid to the generator

[53] See Sections 1.10.1(f), 1.11.3(b), and 3.2.2 of *Appendix to Attachment K of the PJM tariff*

[54] To implement PJM's two-settlement system, modifications were made to Schedule 1 of the Operating Agreement and Appendix K to Attachment K of the PJM tariff, including new provisions re:

- general scheduling (Subsection 1.10.1)
- pool-scheduled resources (Subsection 1.10.2)
- self-scheduled resources (Subsection 1.10.3)
- capacity resources (Subsection 1.10.4)
- external resources (Subsection 1.10.5)
- external market buyers (Subsection 1.10.6)
- bilateral transactions (Subsection 1.10.7)
- office of interconnection responsibilities (Subsection 1.10.8)
- hourly scheduling (Subsection 1.10.9)
- new price calculation provisions
- accounting and billing provisions
- congestion charges and credits provisions

[55] Market participants that deviate from the amounts of energy purchases or sales, or transmission customers that deviate from the transmission uses scheduled in the day-ahead market, are obligated in the real-time market to purchase or sell energy, or pay congestion charges for the amount of the deviation, at the applicable real-time prices or price differences unless otherwise specified

[56] The following explanation is based on PJM's transmittal letter dated March 10, 2000 with respect to its compliance filing in response to FERC's order, referenced below

[57] *PJM Interconnection, L.L.C.*, 86 FERC ¶ 61,147 (1999)

[58] Id. at 61,525

[59] A capacity resource is the net capacity from owned or contracted for generating facilities that are accredited pursuant to the procedures set forth in the Reliability Assurance Agreement. See *PJM tariff* § 1.3c

[60] By basing the day-ahead settlement on day-ahead commitments rather than real-time operations, the two-settlement system removes any incentive that may exist under a single-settlement system for a generator that would be paid its own above-market bid at its minimum load to overstate minimum load requirements. *New England Power Pool*, 87 FERC at 61,192

CHAPTER SIX

Reliability

In Order No. 2000 FERC confirmed that a regional transmission organization (RTO) must have exclusive authority for maintaining the short-term reliability of the grid it operates. Short-term reliability encompasses all RTO transmission responsibilities up to grid capacity enhancement.[1] Short-term reliability responsibilities include:

- exclusive authority for receiving, confirming, and implementing all interchange schedules—a function automatically assumed by RTOs that operate a single control area
- the right to order the re-dispatch of any generator connected to the transmission facilities it operates, if necessary for reliable operation of the transmission system

- when the RTO operates transmission facilities owned by other entities, authority to approve and disapprove all requests for scheduled outages of transmission facilities to ensure that the outages can be accommodated within established reliability standards[2]

In discharging its responsibilities, an RTO must adhere to NERC reliability standards.[3]

In its Order No. 2000 compliance filing, PJM quoted FERC's prior finding that "under the supervision and oversight of the PJM board, [PJM is] responsible for the short-term reliability of the grid."[4] To this end, PJM noted, it coordinates and operates the PJM control area transmission system so that energy transfers do not adversely affect system reliability. PJM operates a single control area and conducts all interchange scheduling for its region. It also has the right to order the re-dispatch of any generator connected to the transmission facilities it operates if necessary for the reliable operation of the transmission system. Finally, PJM has the authority to adjust the output of pool-scheduled resources to serve reliability purposes, including the ability to balance load and generation.

In doing so, PJM constantly monitors transmission transfer capability, which measures the capacity of the transmission system to transfer energy reliably between areas and serves as an indicator to market participants when reserving transmission to schedule energy transactions. PJM calculates transfer capabilities that are commercially viable and provide a reasonable indication of the transfer capability available to the Mid-Atlantic wholesale electric power market for the time period under consideration.[5]

Similar principles are applied for each time frame from the current hour calculation through the 13-month calculation, although different methodologies are used. Whatever the time frame, PJM quantifies available transfer capability (ATC), and total transfer capability (TTC), and posts the results on the PJM OASIS. Since PJM cannot perform ATC analyses on systems external to PJM, transmission customers also review each transmission provider's OASIS to determine what can feasibly be transferred from source to sink across the transmission system. Transmission customers must contract with all applicable control areas along the desired contract path to determine ATC and request transmission service across control areas in addition to PJM's[6] (Table 6-1).

Approval of a transmission request is primarily dependent on ATC and the absence of any known reliability problems. Transmission transfer capability is a measure of the adequacy of the transmission system to reliably transfer energy between areas. In order to ensure system reliability within the PJM control area, the feasibility of transmission service requests is determined by ATC and Total Transfer Capability (TTC).

ATC principles

The PJM OI procedures for determining ATC follow the principles outlined by the North American Electric Reliability Council's (NERC) Transmission Transfer Capability Task Force. They also conform to FERC's final rules.

ATC and TTC calculations are based on NERC–recommended measures, including "First Contingency Incremental Transfer Capability (FCITC)" and "First Contingency Total Transfer Capability (FCTTC)".

(1) FCITC is the amount of electric power (incremental above normal base power transfers) that can be transferred over the interconnected transmission systems in a reliable manner.

(2) FCTTC is the total amount of electric power (net of normal base power transfers plus first contingency incremental transfers) that can be transferred between two areas of interconnected transmission systems in a reliable manner.

The key element in the development of transmission capability for the wholesale electric power market is the total amount of transfer capability available at any given time for purchase or sale. TTC is ATC plus any existing transmission system commitments, including any applicable transfer capability margins and base case adjustments. The calculation of transfer capabilities is based on computer simulations of the operation and response of the interconnected transmission network for a specific set of forecasted operating conditions under three specific time frames:

(1) Near-Term — Hour 0 (current hour) to Hour 168

(2) Mid-Term — 8 to 30 days in the future

(3) Long-Term — 1 to 13 months in the future

Table 6–1 Available Transfer Capacity (ATC)

ATC thus reflects the system's capability to transport or deliver energy above already subscribed transmission uses. To prevent over-commitment and assure system security, PJM preserves a portion of overall transmission network capability to accommodate changes in transmission capability caused by maintenance outages, forced outages of generation and transmission equipment, higher than expected customer loads, shared activation of reserves, and changes in other operating conditions.[7] PJM also determines firm ATC, *i.e.*, the amount of energy above already subscribed firm transmission uses that can be transferred reliably from one control area to another over in-service interconnected transmission facilities in addition to all other known point-to-point and network service reservations.

PJM evaluates transmission service requests to determine system impact and approves or denies the request accordingly. Under the PJM tariff, PJM offers point-to-point and network transmission service and transmission loading relief (TLR) that allows non-PJM transmission service customers to pay through congestion during a TLR event. To become an eligible transmission service customer, an applicant must enter into a Transmission Service Enabling Agreement with PJM. All requests must be posted on PJM's OASIS. PJM then performs ATC calculations.

In determining ATC, PJM includes as constituent factors capacity benefit margin (CBM) and transmission reliability margin (TRM). To serve native load reliably, PJM must have the ability to import external generation and accordingly sets aside a portion of transfer capability. CBM establishes the amount of emergency power that can be reliably transferred to PJM from adjacent regions in the event it suffers a generation capacity deficiency. This transfer limit determines the so-called capacity benefit of ties used in calculating PJM reserve requirements[8] (Table 6-2).

CBM and TRM Components

MARGIN	MARGIN COMPONENTS	NEAR-TERM (Hours 0 – 168)	MID-TERM (Days 8 – 30)	LONG-TERM (Month 2 – 13)
CBM*		PICS Value – Excess Reserve	PICS Value	PICS Value
TRM	LFUM*	2.25% (Hours 0 - 24) 6% (Hours 24 - 168)	6% (Days 8 - 30)	6% (Month 2 - 13)
TRM	ULFM	Historical Path Loop Flow <=5% of Path TTC	Historical Path Loop Flow <=5% of Path TTC	Historical Path Loop Flow <=5% of Path TTC
TRM	NOM	Historical Path Loop Flow <=5% of Path TTC	Historical Path Loop Flow <=5% of Path TTC	Historical Path Loop Flow <=5% of Path TTC

LFUM = Load Forecast Uncertainty Margin
ULFM = Unanticipated Loop Flow Margin
NOM = Normal Operating Margin
PICS = PJM Import Capability Study

*Denotes that total margin is allocated to calculate ATC when PJM is the sink

Table 6–2 CBM and TRM Components

Similarly, to assure secure operation of the interconnected transmission network under a broad range of potential system conditions, PJM sets aside a portion of TRM. TRM provides flexibility for reliable system operations and minimizes the need to curtail transmission service for control purposes. TRM is composed of three constituent elements:

- load forecast uncertainty margin
- loop flow margin
- normal operating margin[9]

Load forecast uncertainty margin reflects PJM's next day or monthly average load forecast error (between 2.25% and 6%) and varies by time frame. Unanticipated loop flow margin addresses the unintended consequences of energy transfers across a network, with consequent adverse impact on system reliability and transfer capability, and is determined by comparing the direction of specific historical path loop flows to those in a base case used to model forecasted system conditions. Normal operating margin is typically 5% of TTC and provides a buffer to avoid the effects on transmission flows of instantaneous changes in load or generation that would occur if the system were scheduled at 100 % of TTC[10] (Fig. 6-1).

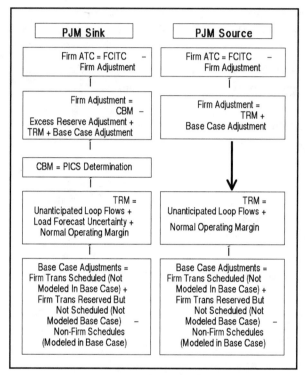

Fig. 6–1 Margin Adjustment for Firm ATC

Interchange scheduling. Because PJM operates a single control area, it conducts all interchange scheduling for its region.[11] As the recipient and evaluator of all requests for transmission service under the PJM tariff, it also receives, confirms, and implements all interchange schedules between adjacent control areas. PJM accommodates pool-scheduled resources (selected on the basis of prices offered for energy, start-up, no-load, and cancellation fees, and specified operating characteristics); self-scheduled resources (which are made available for coordinated operation of supply); capacity resources (which may be either pool-scheduled, self-scheduled, or sold on a bilateral basis); and external resources that specify:

- energy prices
- hours of energy availability and minimum dispatch level

- maximum dispatch level
- flow modeling information
- if resource-specific, the resource being offered[12]

Generation resources are either self-scheduled by load-serving entities within PJM or by PJM itself on a day-ahead or hourly basis. During the scheduling process, PJM determines a plan to serve the hourly energy and reserve requirements of the PJM control area, including the purchase requests of market buyers, in the least costly manner.[13]

In connection with day-ahead scheduling:

- load-serving entities submit forecasts of customer loads for the next operating day, including estimated load curtailment, if any
- market participants that are not load-serving entities submit requests to purchase specified amounts of energy that they intend to purchase on an hourly basis, together with dispatch rate levels above which they will not purchase
- each generating market buyer[14] submits hourly schedules for resource increments, self-scheduled by the market buyer to meet its equivalent load,[15] and the dispatch rate at which each self-scheduled resource will disconnect or reduce output or, in the alternative, confirmation of the market buyer's intent not to reduce output
- all market participants submit schedules for bilateral transactions involving use of generation or transmission facilities and disclose whether the parties to such transactions are not willing to incur transmission congestion charges[16]
- market sellers wishing to sell on the PJM interchange energy market submit offers for the supply of energy, regulation, operating reserves, or other services for the following operating day that:

  ✓ specify the generation resource and energy for each hour in the offer period
  ✓ specify the amounts and prices for the entire operating day for each resource component offered

✓ if based on energy from a specific generating unit, may specify start-up and no-load fees

✓ set forth special conditions, including any curtailment rate specified in a bilateral contract for the output of the resource or any cancellation fees

✓ may include a schedule of offers for prices and operating data contingent on acceptance by the deadline specified in the schedule

✓ constitute an obligation to submit the resource increment for scheduling and dispatch in accordance with the terms proposed, to remain open through the operating day for which the offer is submitted

✓ guarantee final price or prices

✓ do not exceed an energy offer price of $1,000 per megawatt-hour[17]

- a market seller wishing to sell regulation service submits an offer that specifies the number of MW being offered and the applicable regulation class[18]
- a market seller owning or controlling the output of a capacity resource submits a forecast of its availability for the next seven days, each offer of a capacity resource remaining in effect until superseded or canceled
- PJM posts on its OASIS its estimate of market buyers' combined hourly load for the next four days and peak load forecasts for an additional three days[19]

With appropriate notice to PJM, a market participant may also adjust the schedule of a dispatchable resource on an hour-to-hour basis. A generating market buyer may self-schedule a resource not previously self-scheduled or pool-scheduled, may request scheduling of a non-firm bilateral transaction, may request scheduling of deliveries or receipts of spot market energy, or may remove from service a resource previously self-scheduled, subject to PJM's right to schedule energy from a capacity resource at the price offered.[20]

PJM's scheduling plan reflects the most economic means (*i.e.,* least bid prices) of satisfying the projected hourly energy, operating reserve and ancillary services requirements of market buyers[21] consistent with reliability requirements of the PJM control area. In determining the least cost means of doing so, PJM takes into account:

- forecasts of energy requirements, including those submitted by market buyers[22]
- offers submitted by market sellers
- the availability of limited energy resources
- the capacity, location, and other relevant characteristics of self-scheduled resources
- operating reserve requirements
- requirements for regulation and other ancillary services
- the benefits of avoiding or minimizing transmission constraint control operations[23]

In addressing these factors, PJM:

- determines a generation resource schedule to support bilateral sales by and self-scheduling requirements of all PJM members and relieve expected transmission constraints
- performs economic scheduling for load and reserves not otherwise covered by self-scheduled resources and bilateral transactions
- maintains data and information necessary to conduct scheduling and dispatch of the PJM interchange energy market and the PJM control area
- posts its forecast of the location and duration of any expected transmission congestion between areas in the PJM control area
- revises the schedule of generation resources to reflect updated projections of load, changing electric system conditions, and the availability of and constraints on energy and other resources[24]

PJM is thus able to schedule the least-priced generation mix while also maintaining reliability. In doing so, PJM evaluates the price of each available generating unit on a comparative basis until sufficient generation is dispatched in each hour to serve all energy purchase and PJM control area requirements.

To facilitate the scheduling process, PJM employs scheduling tools that permit analysis of differing scheduling scenarios.[25]

PJM members can choose to self-schedule their generation or bid into the market and allow PJM to schedule their generation.[26] PJM members can also purchase generation from the market, depending on their cost of generation and estimate of market price conditions. Each PJM member makes its own choice based on known costs and estimated hourly market prices. PJM selects pool-scheduled resources based on offered energy prices and related services, start-up, no-load, and cancellation fees.[27] A capacity resource selected as a pool-scheduled resource must be made available for scheduling and dispatch at PJM's direction. Energy from a capacity resource not so selected may be sold on a bilateral basis or self-scheduled.[28]

Bilateral transactions are based on agreements between any two entities. Although independent of the spot market, bilateral transactions significantly impact the PJM control area. Requests for bilateral transactions must be submitted before indicated deadlines and contain required data. To support customer choice requirements in an LMP-based market, participants must have the ability to model load apportionment dynamically at buses within the applicable service area. A local distribution company associates each individual retail customer with a specific bus, determines the load apportionment for each alternative supplier, or load aggregator, at each bus, then groups the buses into an aggregate source/sink bus, used in energy schedules and transmission reservations. Aggregate buses include:

- hubs representing a specific region within the PJM control area (*i.e.,* east, west or interface) that reduce volatility, provide a common point for commercial trading, and reveal hub prices as the weighted average LMPs of the buses constituting the hub (Fig. 6-2)
- hubs defined by the eight utility zones making up the PJM control area, with zonal LMP calculated on the basis of weighted loads and sales within each zone
- retail buses defined by local distribution companies to represent the load ownership of a load aggregator within a single zone

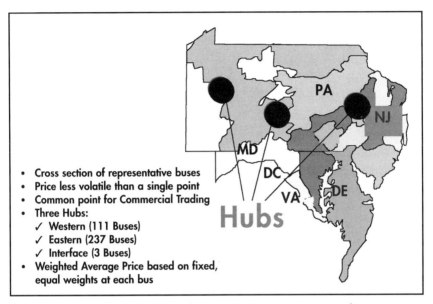

- Cross section of representative buses
- Price less volatile than a single point
- Common point for Commercial Trading
- Three Hubs:
  - ✓ Western (111 Buses)
  - ✓ Eastern (237 Buses)
  - ✓ Interface (3 Buses)
- Weighted Average Price based on fixed, equal weights at each bus

Fig. 6–2 PJM LMP Implementation Training Course Hubs

A valid source and sink must accompany all schedules submitted to PJM. Source and sink data are used to calculate transmission congestion cost every five minutes for approximately 1,600 buses within the PJM control area.[29]

Re-dispatch authority

Under the Operating Agreement, PJM has authority to "schedule and dispatch in real-time generation economically on the basis of least-cost, security-constrained dispatch and the prices and operating characteristic offered by Market Sellers, continuing until sufficient generation is dispatched to serve the PJM Interchange Energy Market energy purchase requirements under normal system conditions of the Market Buyers, as well as the requirements of the PJM Control Area for ancillary services provided by such generation . . ."[30] PJM also has the authority to "adjust the output of pool-scheduled resource increments as necessary to:

- maintain reliability, and subject to that constraint, to minimize the cost of supplying energy, reserves, and other services required by Market Buyers and the operation of the PJM Control Area
- balance load and generation, maintain scheduled tie flows, and provide frequency support within the PJM Control Area
- minimize unscheduled interchange not frequency related between the PJM Control Area and other Control Area"[31]

Dispatching includes system control, ancillary service monitoring, and transmission monitoring and control.[32] During the dispatching process, PJM implements and adjusts its current operating plan, developed during the scheduling process, to maintain reliability and minimize the cost of supplying energy, reserves, and other services (Fig. 6-3, a-b). PJM's dispatching responsibilities include:

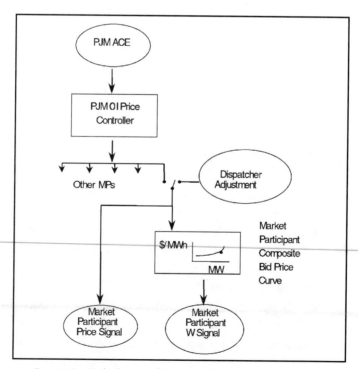

Fig. 6–3a Calculation of Dispatch Price and MW Signals

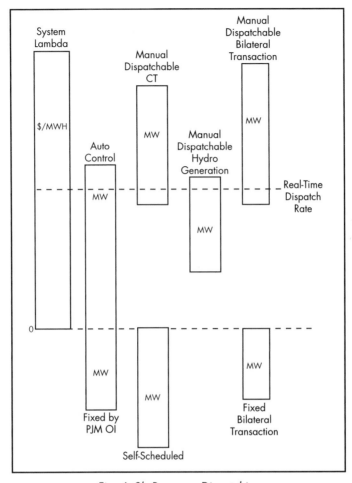

Fig. 6–3b Resource Dispatching

- directing PJM members to adjust the output of any PJM control area-scheduled resource
- canceling selection of any such resource
- operating the PJM control area on a first contingency basis, *i.e.,* operating the bulk power supply system in the PJM control area to protect against the consequences of failure or malfunction of any single bulk power facility so that, immediately following any such failure or malfunction—

✓ the loading on all remaining facilities is within emergency ratings
✓ system stability and an acceptable voltage profile are maintained

• obtaining the most cost-efficient regulation service available
• updating OASIS to reflect PJM's dispatch of generation services

Through its least-cost, security-constrained dispatch and the PJM inter-change energy market, PJM operates a comprehensive system enabling gener-ators to offer their services and permitting PJM to compensate generators that are redispatched for reliability. PJM runs a market in which the generators offer their services and it chooses the least cost options[33] (Fig. 6-4).

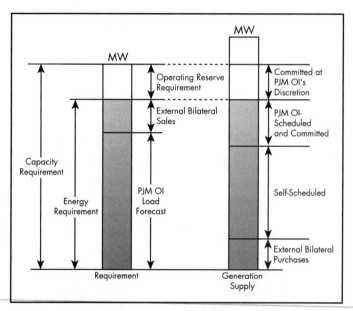

Fig. 6–4 Generation Supply

In addition, PJM is responsible for declaring "the existence of an Emer-gency, and direct[ing] the operations of the Members as necessary to manage, alleviate or end an Emergency."[34] Emergency conditions include an abnormal condition requiring action to maintain system frequency or prevent loss of firm load, equipment damage, or a fuel shortage requiring departure from normal operating procedures. Under certain conditions PJM may curtail or interrupt customer load so there is no cascading loss of transmission facilities.

In the event of an emergency, PJM members must "[c]omply with the requirements of the PJM Manuals and all directives of [PJM] to take any action for the purpose of managing, alleviating or ending an Emergency."[35] These may include load shedding, implementing voltage reductions, and reducing energy purchases. Although the PJM control area is normally loaded according to bid prices, during periods of reserve deficiency PJM may load generation that is restricted for reasons other than cost and take other load relief measures. PJM may also purchase emergency energy from PJM members, who submit bids to supply such energy that are accepted on a least cost, time-ordered basis. Under its organic document, therefore, PJM is accorded control over facilities owned by PJM members, all of which are signatories to the Operating Agreement. In addition, PJM requires all new owners of generation facilities interconnected with the PJM system to execute interconnection service agreements that incorporate the provisions of the Operating Agreement.[36] Finally, PJM responds to requests for general assistance from other control areas based on the APS/PJM/VaPwr Reliability Coordination Plan[37] (Fig. 6-5).

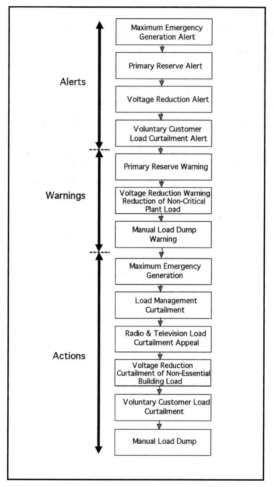

Fig. 6–5 Emergency Levels

Transmission maintenance approval

PJM has authority to approve and disapprove all requests for scheduled outages of transmission facilities to ensure that they can be accommodated within established reliability standards. Under the PJM Operating Agreement, PJM is "responsible for coordinating and approving requests for outages of generation and transmission facilities as necessary for the reliable operation of the PJM Control Area."[38]

Although its members may propose transmission schedules to reflect outages, PJM need not accept them as submitted and may propose alternative schedules. If there are conflicts, PJM resolves them. In sum, PJM receives requests for authorization of preferred maintenance outage schedules, reviews and tests those schedules against reliability criteria, approves specific requests for scheduled outages, requires changes to maintenance schedules when they fail to meet reliability standards, and publishes maintenance schedules as needed.[39]

Generation maintenance approval

PJM also conducts generator-planned outage scheduling for capacity resources. Such outages are typically set well in advance, are of predetermined duration, and include turbine and boiler overhauls, testing, and nuclear refuelings. PJM schedules generation maintenance in accordance with the Reliability Assurance Agreement and the PJM manuals and in consultation with members that own or control the output of capacity resources.

If PJM determines that approval of a generator-planned outage would significantly affect reliable operation of the PJM control area, it may withhold approval or even withdraw a prior approval.[40] If approval is withheld, PJM coordinates with the market participant owning or controlling the resource at the earliest practical time in order to minimize economic impact.

Facility ratings

PJM transmission owners have primary responsibility for calculation of facility ratings based on industry standards, determined using extensive guidelines developed through the PJM committee structure and taking into account PJM's input, local codes, age, and past use of the facilities. PJM tracks and reviews all ratings changes as well as voltage limits within which facilities must operate.[41]

Reliability standards and long-term planning

The Operating Agreement requires PJM to "[c]omply with MAAC and NERC operation and planning standards, principles and guidelines."[42] PJM's manuals, long-term planning, and regional transmission expansion plan (RTEP) must also conform to those standards.[43] PJM has ultimate responsibility for transmission expansion planning in the PJM control area. PJM coordinates regional transmission planning to meet all needs within the region for firm transmission service. Expansion plans emerge from a coordinated process involving the transmission owners for the region and are reviewed publicly through the PJM transmission expansion advisory committee.

The RTEP addresses regional transmission needs of the PJM control area on a consolidated basis. It reflects transmission enhancements and expansions, load and capacity forecasts, generation additions, and retirements for a 10-year period. It also includes a 5-year plan to address near-term expansion or enhancement of the transmission system to meet scheduled in-service dates, primarily related to new merchant plant generation.[44] The present plan reflects interconnection of more than 40 new generating resources to the grid representing over 15,000 MW of new capacity, proposed to be in service by 2005.

The RTEP is required to:

- avoid unnecessary duplication of facilities
- avoid imposition of unreasonable costs on any transmission owner or any user of transmission facilities
- provide alternative means of meeting transmission needs in the PJM control area
- provide for coordination with existing transmission systems and interregional and local expansion plans[45]

Furthermore, PJM's planning and expansion process encourages market-driven operating and investment actions for preventing and relieving congestion. Information regarding constraints and real-time congestion in the system is available to market participants. In determining where to site new generation or increase existing generator capacity, generators can react appropriately to congestion-determined price signals. Moreover, PJM's interconnection procedures assign incremental fixed transmission rights (FTRs) to generators that pay to upgrade the transmission system in order to accommodate interconnection of their generation.[46] Incremental (FTRs) provide an incentive for generators to locate in areas where generation can relieve congestion.

In framing the RTEP, PJM includes independent power producer (IPP) development plans based on specified criteria:

- the IPP developer must be in discussion with PJM and actively pursuing plans for siting generating facilities
- public IPP plans and those of load-serving entities are accorded equal treatment and are explicitly included in the RTEP
- the confidentiality of non-public IPP plans is preserved for such matters as developer's identity and site location
- IPP plans developed as a result of a PJM feasibility study are explicitly evaluated
- IPP plans not so developed are only considered to the extent that new generation may impact transmission expansion alternatives under evaluation

PJM also has an agenda for discussions with regional transmission owners who are expected to disclose the status, impact, and schedule of relevant studies and identify system needs, including new or changing loads that will affect the transmission plan.[47] Finally, PJM has entered into a memorandum of understanding with jurisdictions in the PJM control area to establish a protocol and organizational structure for cooperation.

Reliability Assurance Agreement and Reliability Committee

The Reliability Assurance Agreement (RAA), whose signatories are load-serving entities in the PJM control area, is intended to assure that adequate capacity resources are planned, coordinated, and made available to provide reliable service therein, "consistent with the development of a robust competitive marketplace."[48] The RAA includes procedures to determine the pool-wide generation requirement to meet pool-wide loads, each member's obligation to contribute thereto, compliance with the obligations established, enforcement of a capacity deficiency charge, and adaptation of traditional reserve-sharing within PJM to accommodate introduction of retail choice in the PJM control area.

The RAA is managed and administered by the reliability committee comprising representatives of each party[49] and responsible for:

- approval of the annual forecast pool requirement that establishes the level of installed capacity and reserves required,[50] from a planning perspective, in order to serve load reliably, taking into account unavailability of capacity resources, load forecasting uncertainty, and planned and administrative outages
- approval of the active load management (ALM) factor, which determines the effective capacity value of interrupting ALM customers during emergency conditions as compared to adding resources and serving the higher level of load[51]
- coordination with PJM, the parties to the Operating Agreement, and the Transmission Owners Agreement to:

  ✓ establish the forecast pool requirement for capacity resources
  ✓ establish criteria for use of capacity resources and serving load during emergencies
  ✓ establish the planning period (*i.e.,* the 12 months beginning June 1 and extending through May 31 of the following year)
  ✓ carry out other planning and analyses necessary to satisfy reliability principles and standards

PJM is not a party to the RAA and has only non-voting representation on the reliability committee, which notifies PJM of any decision to fix initially or change the forecast pool requirement for a planning period, the charges for capacity deficiencies, the ALM factor, and the allowable levels of ALM for a party and the PJM control area. The PJM board may request reconsideration of the reliability committee's decision or inability to decide, after which it "shall reconsider the matter or take other appropriate action .

. . [but] [n]o such request shall preclude the PJM Board from advancing any argument it deems appropriate in any other venue to resolve the matter."[52]

The RAA thus places the PJM board in less than a central role, which PJM has characterized as "inconsequential and ineffective" in pleadings filed at FERC.[53] Under the RAA, although the PJM board may provide its views to the reliability committee for its consideration, the reliability committee can unilaterally implement new rules and deprive the PJM board of any means of suspending reliability rules with which it disagrees. In its FERC filing, PJM has criticized this locus of authority: "To . . . allow the load-serving entities that are competing in a newly created competitive market to dictate reliability factors could let short-term economic concerns override long-term reliability and could lead to degradation of system reliability within the PJM Control Area."[54] Specific reliability factors include the level of installed capacity reserves required to serve load reliably system-wide, determination of individual capacity obligations, and calculation of ALM.

To address these concerns PJM has urged FERC to:

- allow the PJM board to cause the immediate suspension of an existing or new reliability rule
- provide that disputes between the PJM board and the reliability committee be resolved under dispute resolution procedures, with ultimate resort to the Commission
- allow the PJM board unilaterally to request the reliability committee to change the reliability rules, subject to dispute resolution
- in emergency situations allow the PJM board unilaterally to place reliability rules in effect without resorting to the reliability committee

Under the RAA, each load-serving entity must own or purchase capacity resources greater than or equal to the load that it serves, plus a reserve margin. As we have seen, PJM periodically forecasts installed capacity needs for the control area to serve load and act as capacity reserves. It allocates to each member that serves load in the control area a portion of the overall capacity requirement. If a member is deficient, it must compensate, at a fixed deficiency charge, other members that have excess capacity.

The RAA therefore requires each load-serving entity to install or contract for capacity resources or obtain capacity credits sufficient to satisfy *each day* its accounted-for obligation. A load-serving entity can do so by relying on its own installed generation, acquiring resource or capacity credits in bilateral markets, or acquiring capacity credits in the PJM capacity credit markets.

Before retail restructuring, the original PJM members determined their loads and related capacity obligations on an annual basis. Each member was required to have installed capacity equal to its load plus a reserve margin or the ability to purchase such capacity. There was also a bilateral secondary market in PJM capacity credits that permitted members short on capacity to buy from members long on capacity. A capacity credit reflected the sale and purchase of rights to capacity for purposes of the PJM capacity obligation. The penalty for being short was the value of newly constructed capacity, based on the cost to build a combustion turbine in the PJM control area. When combined with state regulatory requirements and incentives to maintain adequate capacity, the prior system resulted in a reliable pool, with the cost of capacity obligations borne equitably by members.

Retail restructuring, commenced in 1998, created the opportunity for new entrants to compete to serve retail loads. New entrants wished to acquire capacity to meet loads gained through the competitive process, and the existing utilities wished to sell capacity no longer needed if load were in fact lost to new competitors. In 1999, PJM initiated daily and monthly capacity markets to balance supply and demand for capacity.

As market-based sales of energy were permitted in PJM and surrounding control areas, owners of generation acquired an incentive to sell energy on any given day to the market with the highest price, regardless of location. There is no requirement that generation owners that are not load-serving entities sell capacity to those that serve load in the PJM control area. As a result, under prevailing RAA rules, individual capacity owners may "de-list" capacity and declare that it is no longer a capacity resource and thus cannot be used to meet load-serving entity obligations. Such capacity may therefore be sold off the PJM system. It cannot thereafter be recalled since it is no longer a committed resource. The potential for a generation owner to sell short the PJM system thus increased significantly as utilities divested generation resources and as new competitive entrants assumed obligations to serve load.

Coupled with daily capacity markets to implement retail choice, daily deficiency penalties under the RAA produced flawed incentives. The ability of load-serving entities to meet their annual load obligations in a daily market and the corresponding ability of generators to make a daily decision about whether to sell their capacity to PJM or sell it elsewhere created incentives that diminished the reliability of the PJM system. If forward prices in external energy markets made it profitable for generation owners to sell energy to those markets, generators holding capacity that would otherwise be offered in the daily PJM capacity market were motivated to sell energy in the external markets, thereby depriving load-serving entities of needed capacity and jeopardizing the reliability of the system as a whole. On June 1, 2000, for the first time since introduction of the PJM daily capacity markets in late 1998, total demand for daily capacity credits exceeded the total supply of daily capacity credits, *i.e,* the sum of pool capacity obligations exceeded the sum of capacity made available to PJM.

To address this problem, a PJM stakeholder group propounded modifications to the RAA rules that would require all load-serving entities to meet their obligations to serve load on a long-term basis, instead of a daily basis, by lengthening the capacity commitment term so that a short load-serving entity would be responsible for a deficiency charge for an entire multi-month "interval"—a significant penalty. Load-serving entities would then be required to commit their capacity resources for an entire interval, and deficiency charges would be determined on an interval basis.

The RAA's reliability committee failed to adopt the stakeholder proposal, which required super-majority approval. This caused the PJM board to exercise its authority under Section 206 of the Federal Power Act by petitioning FERC unilaterally in April 2001 to approve the proposed modifications to the RAA, accepted by FERC in June 2001.

Interregional coordination

Order No. 2000 mandates that an RTO "must ensure the integration of reliability practices within an interconnection and market interface practices among regions."[55] FERC's regional approach disregards artificial jurisdictional constraints in order to address uniformly such "seams" problems as parallel path flow, ancillary service standards, transmission loading relief, and inter-regional criteria for calculation of transmission capacity, transmission reservation, scheduling, and congestion management.

To extend its regional scope, PJM has recently entered into a comprehensive affiliation with Allegheny Power System (APS) pursuant to which APS will transfer control of its transmission facilities to PJM, allowing PJM seamlessly to extend its energy market and congestion management across all regions served by both entities. Formation of "PJM West"—a single market embracing multiple control areas—enables PJM to resolve "seams" issues to its west by extending a single LMP-based energy market over multiple control areas.[56] Furthermore, in its July 2001 order provisionally granting PJM RTO status, FERC viewed PJM as the platform for a Northeast RTO encompassing New England and New York.

On March 15, 2001 PJM and APS filed at FERC to establish PJM as the regional transmission organization for APS under the PJM West rubric. Following transfer of control on January 1, 2002, PJM will commence offering service on APS' facilities under the PJM tariff. PJM West will substantially expand the scope of PJM's existing regional market, planning process, and system operations. For the first time, a single regional market with a single congestion management system will cross multiple control areas and multiple regional reliability councils. The resulting wholesale electricity market will be the largest in the world. PJM West will encompass approximately 1.4 million additional end-use customers, 7,800 additional MW of load, 5,000 additional miles of transmission lines and 9,100 additional MW of generation capacity while extending PJM's operations into West Virginia and Ohio. Seams issues along the PJM/APS interface will be eliminated through a common tariff, market, business practices, and customer interface tools. PJM West also contemplates that transmission owners may form an independent transmission company to assume some of the RTO functions otherwise performed by PJM.

The basic agreements establishing PJM West are the PJM West Implementation Agreement (Implementation Agreement),[57] West Transmission Owners Agreement (West TOA),[58] and the PJM West Reliability Assurance Agreement (West RAA). Expansion of PJM also entails amendments to the PJM tariff, Operating Agreement, and TOA. APS and all other interested PJM West market participants are to become signatories to the Operating Agreement and members of PJM. The PJM tariff, including terms, conditions, rules and standards applicable to transmission, ancillary services, market monitoring, and generation interconnection, will apply to the expanded region.[59] The Operating Agreement, including governance rules, interchange energy market rules, congestion management, fixed transmission rights and planning and expansion protocol, will likewise apply to the expanded region. Separate requirements will be continued to account for installed generating capacity and reserves, voltage regulation, and other control area-specific matters:

- Under the West TOA, APS will transfer to PJM responsibility to direct operation of its transmission facilities, provide service under the PJM tariff using those facilities, participate in the RTEP including PJM West, and serve as NERC security coordinator for PJM West.[60] APS also agrees to coordinate its transmission facility maintenance through PJM. The West TOA recognizes that some or all of the PJM West transmission owners may form an independent transmission company to which PJM may transfer certain of its functions, although continuing to act as independent administrator of the regional energy and other markets. The West TOA provides for license plate zonal transmission rate design

- All load serving entities in the PJM West region will become parties to the West RAA, which will be managed by a separate reliability committee under governance and voting rules virtually identical to those in the existing RAA. The West RAA differs from the existing RAA, however, in certain technical and methodological respects. To ensure compatible capacity requirements and a unified energy market as between PJM and PJM West, the West RAA sets an "available capacity" requirement of PJM West of 106% of the next day's forecast peak load, thereby meeting the ECAR daily operating capacity requirement[61]

- The existing Operating Agreement, as amended, will apply to the PJM West control area in addition to the PJM control area. It reflects

- revisions necessary to accommodate technical requirements of the West RAA
- The PJM tariff, as amended, also applies to the PJM West control area and reflects similar technical revisions
- The Implementation Agreement commits PJM to upgrade and expand its systems and facilities as necessary to operate as the regional transmission organization for the PJM West region and to undertake expanded obligations imposed by the West TOA, West RAA, amended Operating Agreement, and amended PJM tariff. The Implementation Agreement also establishes APS' responsibility for PJM's costs to implement PJM West, which APS will recover through transitional charges

When APS joins PJM West, it will become part of a larger integrated system and will be incorporated into PJM's existing approved license-plate rate design, thereby eliminating rate pancaking across a large region. Upon joining PJM, APS' system will become a zone within PJM, with individual zonal rates similar to those used by PJM's current transmission-owning members. Upon joining PJM West, APS will collect no revenues from APS-PJM transactions and will suffer reduced revenues from transactions going through or out of APS. The revenue shortfall will be made up through certain transitional charges. Upon creation of the PJM RTO, certain APS transmission contracts will be grandfathered. PJM's governance structure will be unchanged. It will continue to be governed by its independent, non-stakeholder board of managers, and APS and other interested PJM West market participants will become members of PJM. PJM will also apply to PJM West the same operational authority and responsibility for short-term reliability, tariff administration, congestion management, ancillary services, market monitoring, planning, and expansion as are in effect in PJM.

PJM and PJM West combined will serve 11 million customers in all of the District of Columbia, Delaware and Maryland; nearly all of New Jersey and Pennsylvania; large portions of West Virginia; and parts of Virginia and Ohio. PJM will operate 13,100 miles of transmission lines with a total transfer capability of 13,000 MW and dispatch almost 600 generating units with installed capacity of more than 66,000 MW.

Even prior to FERC's July 2001 RTO order, PJM's influence also extended eastward to ISO New England, which proposed to FERC a comprehensive standardized wholesale market program including salient features of the PJM market model.[62] In close collaboration with PJM and a joint systems contractor, ALSTOM ESCA, ISO New England contemplated a standard market design for wholesale electricity markets to reduce risk, reduce support and maintenance costs, facilitate transactions through uniform market rules, and provide nearly 100% convergence between PJM and ISO New England. Implementing the standard market design presupposed adoption of PJM's market rules, operating practices, and use of three primary pieces of PJM software: its external transaction software, locational marginal pricing calculator, and its dispatch management tool. ISO New England would also acquire rights to PJM's settlement system.

PJM has also been actively involved in interregional cooperation among ISOs in the eastern interconnection. In 1999 PJM entered into a memorandum of understanding with ISO New England, the New York ISO, and Ontario's Independent Electricity Market Operator with a view to:

- enhancing bulk power supply reliability by increasing intertie capacity as part of regional transmission planning
- facilitating broader competitive markets by identifying and addressing market interface constraints
- establishing working groups to address the interregional implications of operations, planning, business practices, communications, and information technology

The working groups have been the backbone of the joint coordination effort. The operations working group seeks to implement uniform procedures for confirming transactions and schedules among control areas and for handling dispatchable contracts. The planning working group is charged with enhancing overall coordination of interregional planning. The business practices working group is intended to create a virtual ISO encompassing all four signatories to the memorandum of understanding, including seamless transaction management across the extended region, region-wide congestion management procedures, and uniform business practices. The communications working group fosters enhanced interaction among market participants and stakeholders through improved communication and feedback mechanisms, while the information technology working group applies emerging technology solutions to common regional problems.

Interregional planning requires, among other things, that ISOs within a region identify generation projects having an impact on neighboring systems. A coordinated planning effort must address such complex issues as milestone requirements and the rights of project developers holding places in multiple ISO interconnection queues, improvement in planning tools, expansion of transmission system capability for both reliability and economic purposes, and "seams" issues, including harmonization of the differing procedures and practices of adjacent ISOs as to such matters as generation interconnection, capacity resource planning, transmission expansion planning, and curtailment and cancellation of scheduled transactions.

PJM and NEPOOL have also entered into an Emergency Reliability Service Agreement to preserve the reliability of their respective electric systems, which are indirectly interconnected so that operations in one control area may affect operations in the other. In emergency situations, NEPOOL may import energy from Hydro-Quebec over high voltage direct current wires. When this happens, PJM may confront instantaneous power flows if NEPOOL suffers a sudden operational loss. To meet this concern the Emergency Reliability Service Agreement provides that, upon NEPOOL's request under emergency conditions, PJM may adjust its dispatch to accommodate operation of the NEPOOL control area. PJM also has agreements with Allegheny Power, Virginia Electric and Power Company, Cleveland Electric Illuminating Company the New York ISO under which PJM will provide emergency service to interconnected control areas[63] (Fig 6-6).

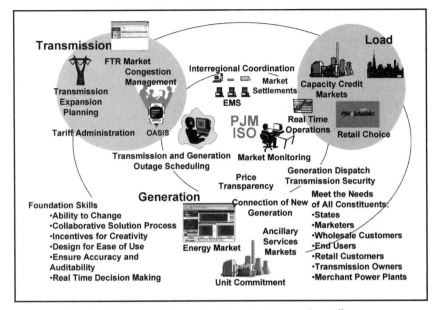

Fig. 6–6 Dynamic Operation Through Independent Efficiency

Transmission enhancement

As we have seen, transmission expansion planning is a key element of long-term reliability. In response to FERC's invitation in Order No. 2000, the PJM transmission owners submitted as part of PJM's compliance filing, a transmission enhancement and innovative rate proposal.[64] If implemented, the proposal will provide incentives to facilitate transmission investment in the PJM control area, including concrete commitments by the PJM transmission owners to undertake PJM-directed grid enhancements and innovative rate treatments.

The proposal has the following features:

- The PJM transmission owners commit to initiate projects they are required to construct pursuant to the regional transmission expansion plan (RTEP) in their respective zones within 90 days of receiving notice from the PJM board that the proposed facilities are acceptable, whether or not there is final agreement on allocation of costs. All PJM transmission owners commit to share jointly funding responsibility for high voltage facilities on a load-weighted basis.[65] They also commit to own the resulting facilities jointly as tenants in common and provide management by contract to address financial, construction, and maintenance functions[66]

- PJM transmission owners contemplate construction of economic transmission enhancements, not required by the RTEP, where such enhancements relieve congestion uniquely affecting particular customers. If those customers are willing to bear the cost of transmission upgrades, PJM transmission owners propose to build them, subject to PJM's approval and negotiated contracts under which the customers agree to provide fair compensation. Given the reliability aspects of transmission expansion in PJM, local issues of siting and licensing and transmission's regulated monopoly status, most new investment in transmission will continue to be governed by rate-based and cost-based regulation. At the same time, through locational marginal pricing, PJM's market-oriented solution to managing grid congestion, market participants can quantify congestion costs and thereby agree on a market-based transmission fix

- Transmission enhancement is also encouraged through innovative rate elements consistent with Order No. 2000, including a transmission rate moratorium through December 31, 2004, extension of zonal rates within PJM through the same time period, deferred cost recovery, accelerated depreciation (15-year life) and risk-adjusted rate of return provisions for transmission investments, and extension of zonal rates within PJM.[67] The accounting adjustments are deemed essential since PJM transmission owners would under the proposal agree to forego their right to increase payments immediately to cover the cost of significant capital expenditures. The proposal does not recommend specific rates of return for new transmission investment since such rates are deemed to be project-specific. A rate moratorium is commonly regarded as the equivalent of a first-generation performance-based rate plan (PBR).[68] To develop a definitive PBR recommendation, the PJM transmission owners would seek to establish measurable benchmarks during the moratorium period. After the moratorium ends on December 31, 2004, the PJM transmission owners could incorporate recovery of deferred capital costs in their transmission rates, subject to an appropriate post-moratorium rate methodology

- To implement the foregoing changes, the PJM transmission owners and PJM proposed to amend the Transmission Owners Agreement (TOA) by making PJM a signatory for certain purposes, clarifying the relationship between PJM and the PJM transmission owners, memorializing the latter's commitment to build transmission enhancements according to prescribed standards, requiring the start of construction activities within 90 days after notification of PJM board approval, and confirming PJM's right to enforce transmission commitment and obligation to make payments for use of transmission facilities. The PJM transmission owners would continue to have the right and responsibility to make Section 205 filings as to compensation received for permitting PJM to provide access to their transmission facilities under the PJM tariff

The foregoing transmission expansion plan and incentive rate proposal were rejected by FERC in its July 2001 order provisionally granting RTO status to PJM. FERC noted that PJM's transmission owners, as market participants, continue to maintain rights relating to reliability, interconnection, and transmission expansion that are not held by other market participants. While generally supportive of the types of incentives offered by the transmission owners, FERC viewed their proposal as a unilateral filing and concluded that PJM, as RTO, must be responsible for developing the transmission enhancement plan and related pricing proposals.

Long-term generating capacity

PJM's long-term reliability functions also involve a planning procedure for generating capacity that begins well in advance of need in order to allow for site preparation, fuel supplies, and construction. In a span of more than two years,

PJM obtains load forecasts from load-serving entities to assist it in determining peak load demand for a given planning period; establishes the reserve requirement for the PJM control area based on NERC and MAAC standards and its own reliability analysis;[69] and determines the overall generating capacity requirement with respect to each load-serving entity. Each load-serving entity must submit its plans for providing its share of the overall requirement through installation of new capacity and purchases of capacity from non-load-serving entities and load-serving entities with excess capacity (Fig. 6-7).

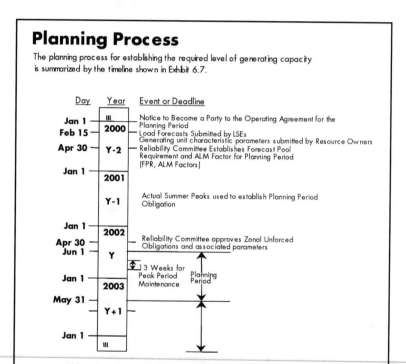

Planning Process

The planning process for establishing the required level of generating capacity is summarized by the timeline shown in Exhibit 6.7.

Day	Year	Event or Deadline
Jan 1	ιιι	Notice to Become a Party to the Operating Agreement for the Planning Period
Feb 15	2000	Load Forecasts Submitted by LSEs
		Generating unit characteristic parameters submitted by Resource Owners
Apr 30	Y-2	Reliability Committee Establishes Forecast Pool Requirement and ALM Factor for Planning Period (FPR, ALM Factors)
Jan 1	2001	
	Y-1	Actual Summer Peaks used to establish Planning Period Obligation
Jan 1	2002	
Apr 30		Reliability Committee approves Zonal Unforced Obligations and associated parameters
Jun 1	Y	
		3 Weeks for Peak Period Maintenance — Planning Period
Jan 1	2003	
May 31	Y+1	
Jan 1	ιιι	

Where Y represents the first year of the Planning Period.

The generating capacity planning procedure begins well in advance of the applicable planning period to allow for site preparation, fuel supply procurement, and construction. The timeline above shows the sequence of actions for the 2002/2003 Planning Period.

Fig. 6–7 PJM Generating Capacity Requirements Timeline

The amount of generating capacity required for the PJM control area depends on the expected customer load forecast and the related reserve established by PJM. The calculation process for determining the pool requirement involves the following principal elements:

- Diversified planning period peak—seasonal peak load forecast and generator unit capability
- Forecast pool requirement—diversified planning period peak x (1 + % PJM reserve margin/100)
- Forecast LSE obligation
- Accounted-for obligation—used to determine if a load-serving entity is deficient and has incurred deficiency charges based on the difference between actual and forecast conditions (Fig. 6-8)

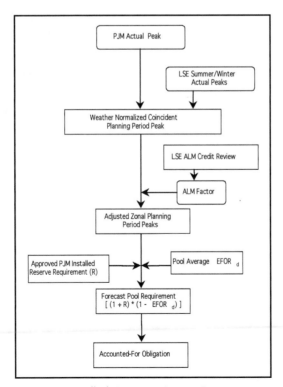

Fig. 6–8 Installed Capacity System Requirements

Based on the foregoing data, PJM performs an annual reliability analysis that calculates the PJM control area reserve requirement, including forced outage rate adjustment and active load management. From these inputs PJM establishes the overall generating capacity requirement for each load-serving entity. The primary analytic tool is a probabilistic computer program that takes into account loss-of-load expectation of up to two interconnected systems with a single transfer link and installed capacity reserve needed to provide a user-specified level of reliability. The program entails computer modeling to describe customer load demand pattern and generating capacity available over the time period of the reliability study. Special rules apply to such limited energy resources as run-of-river hydroelectric power and pumped storage.

Generating capacity is required not only to meet load demand but also to provide for a reliability cushion in the event of unforeseen circumstances, such as the sudden loss of a generating unit. To address this concern, PJM performs an analysis that determines an import value, expressed in MW, for each load-serving entity and measures it against an applicable emergency transfer limit. The transfer limit must be equal to or greater than the import value to satisfy reliability requirements. A capacity credit is available for external purchases, *i.e.*, purchases from generating units located outside the PJM control area. For this and other purposes, PJM takes into account the availability of transmission capacity.

Notes

[1] *Order No. 2000,* at 31,103; 18 C.F.R. § 35.34(j)(4)(2000)

[2] Id. at 31,104-06. FERC found that two other characteristics—generator maintenance approval and establishment of facility ratings—are desirable but unnecessary for RTO status

[3] Id. at 31,106

[4] *PJM ISO Order,* 81 FERC at 62,266

[5] *PJM Manual for Transmission Service Request (Manual M-02, Revision 05)* dated June 2, 1999, pp. 2-10. The PJM operations planning department is responsible for calculation of near-, mid-, and long-term ATC. Calculation of transfer capabilities is based on computer simulations of the operation and response of the interconnected transmission network for a specific set of forecasted operating conditions under specific time frames: Near-term (hour 0 to hour 168); mid-term (8 to 30 days in the future); and long-term (1 to 13 months in the future). The assumptions and projections form the starting point for the transfer analysis. A power flow solution is applied to this starting point to determine the projected power transfer from a source area to a sink area based on an economic generation dispatch. The transfer capability of the network is determined for each posted path, sequentially, by varying the source area generation and sink area load until a system constraint is reached in accordance with PJM operating criteria. Once a limit is encountered, the transfer capability of the network is known, and from this point the ATC and TTC of the specific posted path are determined arithmetically. Id. at 2-15

[6] Id. at 2-11

[7] Id. at 2-26

[8] Id. at 2-27

[9] Id. at 2-26-29

[10] Id. at 2-28-29

[11] Schedule 1 to *PJM Operating Agreement* § 1.10

[12] Schedule 1 to *PJM Operating Agreement* §§ 1.10.2-5

[13] *PJM Manual for Scheduling Operations (Manual M-11, Revision 07)* dated June 1, 1999, p. 1-1

[14] Section 1.3.6 of Schedule 1 to the *PJM Operating Agreement* defines *generating market buyer* to mean an internal market buyer that is a load-serving entity that owns or has contractual rights to the output of generation resources capable of serving the market buyer's load in the PJM control area or selling energy or related services in the PJM interchange energy market or elsewhere

[15] Section 1.3.2 of Schedule 1 to the *PJM Operating Agreement* defines *equivalent* load to mean the sum of a market participant's net system requirements to serve its customer load in the PJM control area, if any, plus its net bilateral transactions

[16] Internal market buyers submit schedules for all bilateral purchases for delivery within the PJM control area, whether from generation resources inside or outside the PJM control area. Market sellers submit schedules for bilateral sales to entities outside the PJM control area that are not dynamically scheduled to those entities. Market participants also submit confirmations of each scheduled bilateral transaction from each party to the transaction

[17] Schedule 1 to *PJM Operating Agreement*, § 1.10.1

[18] Section 1.3.32 of Schedule 1 to the PJM Operating Agreement defines *regulation class* to mean a subset of the generation units capable of providing regulation top the PJM control area determined by a range of costs for providing regulation

[19] Schedule 1 of *PJM Operating Agreement*, § 1.10.1

[20] Id. at § 1.10.9

[21] There are two general types of market buyers. A metered market buyer purchases energy from the PJM interchange energy market for consumption by end-users located inside the PJM control area or owns or has contractual rights to the output of generation resources capable of serving the market buyers' load in the PJM control area or selling energy-related services in the PJM interchange energy market or elsewhere. A metered market buyer must submit to PJM forecasts of customer load for the next operating day; economic load management agreements; hourly schedules for self-scheduled resource increments; a forecast of the availability of each capacity resource for the next seven days. and offer data for capacity resources for supply of energy to the PJM interchange energy market for the next day. An unmetered market buyer makes purchases of energy from the PJM interchange energy market for consumption by metered end-users located outside the PJM control area. An unmetered market buyer's scheduling responsibilities include submission of optional requests to purchase specified amounts of energy for each hour of the operating day and the purchase of transmission capacity reservation in order to receive generation from the PJM interchange energy market. Id. at pp. 1-4-5

[22] Each PJM member serving load within the PJM control area provides PJM with a day-ahead forecast of its requirements. PJM compares the forecasts submitted by PJM members against its own control area load forecast, which takes precedence over the aggregate of individual forecasts in the event of a discrepancy

[23] *PJM Operating Agreement*, Schedule 1 § 1.10.8(a)

[24] Id. at pp. 1-3

[25] Scheduling tools include the Accounting Contracts and Energy Schedules (ACES) program, PJM eSchedules, Load Forecasting Algorithms, Unit Commitment Data Management System, Hydro Calculator, Marginal Scheduler, and Transmission Outage Data System.

Together these tools recognize reactive limits, unit constraints, unscheduled power flows, inter-area transfer limits, unit distribution factors, self-scheduled resources, limited fuel resources, bilateral transactions, hydrological constraints, generation requirements, and reserve requirements. Id. at 2-2

[26] *PJM Operating Agreement,* Schedule 1 § 1.10.1-3

[27] Id. at § 1.10.1

[28] Id. at § 1.10.4. As defined in §1.6, a *capacity resource* means the net capacity from owned or contracted for generating facilities all of which are accredited to a load-serving entity pursuant to the Reliability Assurance Agreement and are committed to satisfy the load-serving entity's obligations thereunder

[29] See *PJM Manual for Scheduling Operations,* pp. 3-17-18

[30] Under Section 1.3.25 of the Operating Agreement, "'PJM Interchange' shall mean the following, as determined in accordance with the Schedules to this Agreement: (a) for a Market Participant that is a Network Service User, the amount by which its hourly Equivalent Load exceeds, or is exceeded by, the sum of the hourly outputs of its operating generating resources; or (b) for a Market Participant that is not a Network Service User, the amount of its Spot Market Backup; or (c) the hourly scheduled deliveries of Spot Market Energy by a Market Seller from an External Resource; or (d) the hourly net metered output of any other Market Seller; or (e) the hourly scheduled deliveries of Spot Market Energy to an External Market Buyer; or (f) the hourly scheduled deliveries to an Internal Market Buyer that is not a Network Service User"

[31] Id. at § 1.11.1

[32] The PJM control area must operate sufficient generating capacity under automatic control to meet its obligation to continuously balance its generation and interchange schedules with its load and to satisfy its frequency regulation obligation as a member of the eastern interconnection. NERC establishes definitive measures of control performance. PJM sends regulation and dispatch control signals to each PJM member whose generating resources come under PJM's direction. PJM is responsible for monitoring reserves to determine undergeneration or overgeneration and adjusts spinning reserves accordingly. PJM also obtains the most cost-efficient regulation ancillary service available, as needed to meet the PJM control area's regulating requirement. To address transmission problems, such as overloads, excessive transfers and low/high voltage conditions, PJM may implement various corrective strategies, including reactive limitation control, voltage control, transaction curtailment, changes in on/off cost operating modes, selected unit adjustment, adoption of NERC transmission loading relief procedure, and implementation of a reliability coordination plan. See *PJM Manual for Dispatching Operations,* Sections 3-5

[33] See *Order No. 2000,* at 31,104

[34] *PJM Operating Agreement* § 10.4(xx)

[35] Id. at § 11.3.1(e)

[36] See, *e.g., PJM Interconnection, L.L.C.,* Docket Nos. ER00-2906-000, 001 (Aug. 16, 2000)

[37] See *PJM Manual for Emergency Operations,* Section 4-2

[38] *PJM Operating Agreement,* Schedule 1 § 1.9.1

[39] *Order No. 2000,* at 31,005

[40] *PJM Operating Agreement,* Schedule 1 § 1.9.2(b)

[41] *PJM Interconnection, L.L.C.,* 92 FERC ¶ 61,186 (2000)

[42] *PJM Operating Agreement* § 10.4(iv)

[43] *PJM Operating Agreement,* Schedule 1 § 1.7.14; Schedule 6 § 1.2(c). Schedule 6 sets forth the regional transmission planning protocol for the PJM control area. The protocol "generally adopts the NERC and MAAC criteria, obligates the [PJM Transmission Owners] to supply staff, data and systems to support regional analysis and provides for participation of all interested parties including regulatory agencies and consumer advocates in affected states, as well as coordination with neighboring control area." *PJM ISO Order,* 81 FERC at 62,275 (finding regional transmission expansion plan reasonable). Under the protocol, PJM "shall prepare the Regional Transmission Expansion Plan, which shall consolidate the transmission needs of the region into a single plan which is assessed on the basis of maintaining the PJM Control Area's reliability in an economic and environmentally acceptable manner." Schedule 6 § 1.4(a)

[44] *PJM Operating Agreement,* Schedule 6 § 1.4(b)

[45] Id. at § 1.4(d)

[46] *PJM's Order No. 2000 Compliance Filing* dated October 11, 2000; mimeo, p. 54

[47] See, *e.g., 1998-99 PJM Regional Transmission Plan Scope and Procedure*

[48] *Reliability Assurance Agreement,* Article 2

[49] PJM is entitled to appoint a non-voting representative to the reliability committee pursuant to Section 6.1.1 of the RAA

[50] The Operating Agreement permits PJM members to meet part of their installed capacity obligations by means of generating units located outside the PJM control area, *i.e.,* an external capacity resource. The capacity value of such a resource is converted into an installed capacity value, discounted to reflect use of existing PJM's emergency import capability. *PJM Reserve Manual* § 3-14

[51] Id. at § 6.2 and 7.1

[52] *Reliability Assurance Agreement,* § 6.4.3

[53] See *Motion to Intervene and Protest of PJM Interconnection, L.L.C.* filed in Docket No. ER98-3457-000 dated July 10, 1998

[54] Ibid; mimeo, at p. 13

[55] 18 C.F.R. § 35.34(k)(7)(ii)(2000)

[56] See *PJM Interconnection, L.L.C. and the Allegheny Power System operating companies: Monongahela Power Company, The Potomac Edison Company, and West Penn Power Company, all doing business as Allegheny Power,* FERC Docket Nos. ER01 and EC01 (March 15, 2001); continued in Docket No. RTO 1-98.

[57] The Implementation Agreement will terminate once PJM becomes the transmission provider for Allegheny's facilities and is in the nature of a precedent agreement

[58] The West TOA is PJM Rate Schedule FERC No. 33

[59] Allegheny contemplates recovery of lost transmission revenues ($27.7 million) from the elimination of rate pancaking and addition of transitional charges on all "through" and "out" firm and non-firm point-to-point service

[60] West TOA, §§ 2.3.4-7, 4.8

[61] West RAA, § 8.1 and Schedule 3, paragraph A

[62] See letter filed in Docket No. RM99-2-000 on March 29, 2001 and accompanying report

[63] See *PJM Interconnection L.L.C.,* Docket No. ER99-4227-000, Letter Order (Sept. 27, 1999)

[64] Under Order No. 2000, 18 C.F.R. § 35.34(e)(2)(2000), such a proposal may have a variety of components, including a transmission rate moratorium, incentive rates of return, non-traditional depreciation schedules, transmission rates based on levelized recovery of capital costs, or transmission rates that combine elements of incremental cost pricing for new transmission facilities with an embedded-cost access fee for existing transmission facilities

[65] Proposed Transmission Owners Agreement Section 7.1

[66] This is consistent with the historical practice in the PJM region of managing through contractual vehicles such as the Extra High Voltage Facilities Agreement of 1967, the Lower Delaware Valley Agreement of 1977, the Susquehanna-Eastern Agreement of 1976, and the Transmission Enhancement Facilities Agreement of 1983

[67] *PJM tariff, Attachment H. See also* Section 35.34(e) of the Commission's regulations, Order No. 2000, at 31,194 ("[W]e believe that it is appropriate for the Commission to provide those willing to make new transmission investments with the flexibility to propose that such assets follow non-traditional depreciation schedules."). *Cf. Southern California Edison Co.,* 92 FERC ¶ 61,070 (2000) (rate of return)

[68] See *Makholm, Assessment of PJM Transmission Owners' Transmission Enhancement Package,* filed at FERC on October 11, 2000 in connection with PJM's RTO compliance filing

[69] A capacity credit is available for external purchases. MAAC and PJM reserve requirements are defined as the level of installed reserves needed to maintain the desired reliability index of 10 years per day (loss of load expectation of one day every 10 years). *PJM Manual M-20 (PJM Reserve Requirements)* (August 19, 1999), p. 3-11

CHAPTER SEVEN

Generator Interconnections and Operations

Just as PJM undertakes transmission planning, it also coordinates the reliable supply of energy from generating units to wholesale customers. This includes the planning process for new generation built in PJM's control area. Generators in PJM may:

- sell generation directly into PJM and receive payment at the locational marginal price
- sell capacity as a separate product directly to load serving entities or through the capacity credit market
- sell regulation into the market-based regulation market and participate in future ancillary services markets
- sell energy to areas outside PJM
- self-schedule generation to serve load obligation

All generators interconnected with and synchronized to the grid must coordinate their operations with PJM and the local control center, while conforming to applicable reliability criteria.

Part IV of the PJM tariff describes the expansion and upgrade process for generation interconnections, including the rules for making an interconnection request, the various studies required to determine necessary interconnection facilities and cost responsibility for facilities and upgrades. The PJM tariff describes how PJM manages this process with the support of transmission owners in performing the necessary feasibility and system impact studies.

New or changed generation

Because PJM's grid is interconnected and balanced, introduction of new generation or change in the output of existing generation within the PJM control area is subject to a formalized administrative procedure (Fig. 7-1). New generation applicants may request either capacity or energy-only service. The latter allows the generator to participate in PJM's energy markets based on locational marginal prices, while the former allows the generator to be used by load-serving entities to meet capacity obligations imposed under the Reliability Assurance Agreement. Capacity resources may also participate in PJM capacity credit markets and ancillary services markets.

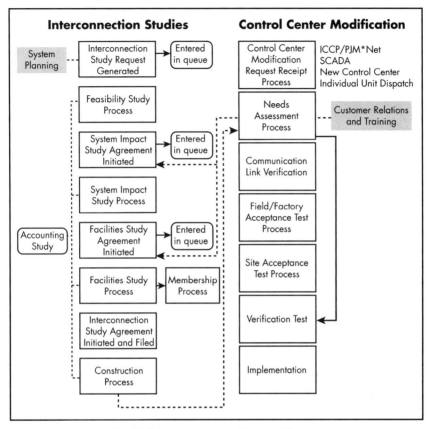

Fig. 7–1 Interconnection Process Diagram

A party wishing to connect new generation to the PJM system must submit an interconnection request in the form of an executed feasibility study agreement and a non-refundable deposit of $10,000. The agreement must include descriptions of project location, size and equipment configuration, proof of the applicant's right to control the proposed project site, and an anticipated in-service date, which must be no later than seven years after the application date unless it is demonstrated that engineering, permitting, and construction of the project will require additional time. Upon its receipt, the interconnection request is placed in a queue, based on the date of its submission.

New owners of existing generation must execute an interconnection service agreement with PJM. Transfer of ownership of existing generation units is not subject to the queue, unless pre-existing capacity injection rights for the unit in question are not transferred with the change of ownership. However, an increase in the output capability of an existing unit is treated as new generation for administrative compliance purposes.

Feasibility studies

Upon receipt of the interconnection request, PJM conducts the required feasibility study, usually within 30 days, to assess the practicality and cost of new or increased generation capacity. The study includes preliminary estimates of the type, scope, cost, and lead time for construction of facilities required to interconnect the project. Results are published on PJM's website, which identifies the location of the project and its size in MW but keeps the applicant's identity confidential.

The applicant must decide whether or not to complete a system impact study. If the applicant elects to proceed, it must submit an executed system impact study agreement with a $50,000 deposit, evidence of required air permits, and a declaration whether the project is to be connected as a capacity or energy-only resource.

System impact studies

To maintain its assigned priority in the queue, an applicant must enter into a system impact study agreement and submit the related deposit within 30 days of receiving the agreement. Failure to meet the deadline terminates the interconnection request. Typically, PJM completes the study within 120 days to provide a comprehensive regional analysis of the impact of adding new generation to the system and an evaluation of its deliverability to PJM load. The study also identifies project-related system constraints, required local and network upgrades, and the relationship between the applicant's generation and that of other generators in the queue.

Facilities Studies

Completion of a facilities study to document necessary engineering design work and provide a cost estimate for upgrades is the final step in the planning process. The applicant must enter into a facilities study agreement and provide a deposit of $100,000 or the amount of the applicant's cost responsibility for the study, whichever is greater.

Interconnection service agreement

Upon completion of the facilities study, PJM furnishes the applicant with an interconnection service agreement (ISA) determining the applicant's cost responsibility for required transmission system upgrades, confirming the applicant's rights as either a capacity or energy-only source, and imposing operational restrictions and limitations as applicable. Within 60 days the applicant must execute and return ISA, request dispute resolution, or request that the ISA be filed with FERC unexecuted.[1] In any event, the applicant must provide PJM acceptable security in an amount equal to the cost of new facilities or upgrades for which the applicant is contractually responsible. The applicant must also demonstrate that it has:

- entered into fuel delivery and water agreements, as applicable
- acquired rights-of-way for fuel and water interconnections
- acquired necessary local, county and state site permits
- entered into preliminary agreements for acquisition of major equipment, such as turbine generators

Typically, the applicant will also indicate milestone dates for permitting, regulatory certifications, and fulfillment of conditions imposed by third-party financial arrangements.[2]

Metering requirements

All generators connecting to the PJM system are required to install and operate metering equipment capable of recording and transmitting voice and data communications. Generators of 10 MW or more must supply real-time and revenue information through the local utility or by direct connection. Real-time information is collected at a two-second data rate, and revenue information is collected hourly. The revenue information is necessary to meet the requirements of PJM's market settlements program, and the real-time information to provide input to the state estimator and other energy management applications.

Capacity performance related requirements

A generator serving as a capacity resource must submit design data to PJM, initially on paper, with performance data later submitted electronically through the PJM generator availability data system (eGADS), which allows generators to access outage and performance data. PJM uses a 12-month history from eGADS to calculate the demand equivalent forced outage rate (EFORd) for each generating unit—a measure of a unit's availability used to convert its installed capacity rating to an unforced capacity rating for the purpose of PJM's capacity markets.[3]

Influence of transmission owners

In its July 2001 order provisionally granting RTO status to PJM, FERC noted the influence of transmission owners over the generation interconnection process in setting priorities, determining needed facilities, and assigning costs as a means of shaping the process to favor their competitive interests. Since many transmission owners also own significant generation capacity within the PJM control area, FERC viewed such influence as a deterrent to future expansion and determined that the entire interconnection process must be under PJM's sole decisional control as

RTO, *i.e.,* customers must deal with and sign interconnection and study agreements with PJM alone.

Energy markets

As noted, PJM operates a wholesale energy market, a regulation market, a capacity credit market, and an ancillary services market, each of which constitutes a marketing option available to generator owners within the PJM control area (although not every generating unit qualifies to participate in each market).

- The PJM wholesale energy market includes both day-ahead and real-time balancing markets. In the day-ahead market locational marginal prices are calculated for each hour of the next operating day based on generation offers, demand bids, and bilateral transaction schedules submitted in advance. The next-day schedule uses least cost, security-constrained unit commitment, and security-constrained economic dispatch programs. By entering the day-ahead market, generators may commit to energy prices and transmission congestion charges in advance of real-time dispatch and may submit price-sensitive demand bids, increment offers, decrement bids, and caps on the maximum congestion charges it is willing to pay. Settlements take place separately in each market.
- The PJM regulation market comprises both day-ahead and balancing markets, and provides a market-based system for the purchase and sale of regulation as an ancillary service allowing a generator to increase or decrease its output in response to a regulating control signal. PJM combines unit-specific regulation offers submitted by generators with forecast locational marginal prices and generation schedules to calculate an hourly, day-ahead regulation market clearing price—used to determine the credits awarded to providers and charges allocated to purchasers of the regulation service.
- Generators serving as capacity resources may submit bids to the PJM daily capacity credit market or the longer-term capacity credit market

using eCapacity, an electronic tool, to create bilateral capacity transactions or submit capacity modifications to increase or decrease the installed capacity rating of a unit.

- Ancillary services include:

  ✓ scheduling, system control, and dispatch service
  ✓ RTO scheduling, system control, and dispatch service
  ✓ reactive supply and voltage control from generation sources service
  ✓ regulation and frequency response service
  ✓ energy imbalance service
  ✓ operating reserves

PJM's Tariff allows customers the option to self-supply or acquire ancillary services from third parties as Order No. 2000 requires. Consistent with that Order, however, PJM is the provider of last resort for all required ancillary services. It can decide the minimum required amounts of ancillary services and where those services must be provided. As we have seen, PJM does so in the context of operating a real-time balancing market and an interchange energy market while providing energy imbalance and operating reserves at market-based rates.

Marketing tools

All electricity transactions within the PJM control area take place on PJM's web site. Membership in PJM is required to buy and sell through the site. PJM maintains a database containing relevant generator information (owner, plant, operating limits, and unit availability) allowing PJM to pre-schedule, schedule, and dispatch generation within the PJM control area. Generators may initially submit cost-based or price-based bids to PJM. All generators also must have a cost-capped bid on file. After a price-based bid has been submitted, the generation owner cannot return to cost-based bidding for that unit.

- PJM eSchedules was PJM's first Internet-based application and drives its wholesale energy market. All power marketers, load-serving entities, and generation owners submit their internal energy schedule data using PJM eSchedules, which includes all PJM internal transactions, including load and generation interchange adjustment modeling and implicit internal spot market schedules. With this tool, users can determine, in real time, whether the transmission system can accommodate a specific transaction.
- PJM eCapacity manages the capacity market and enables utilities and load aggregators to match excess capacity with capacity shortfalls. Users can view peak loads and obligations in any zone, shop for PJM installed capacity, and create bilateral transactions to buy or sell unit-specific or capacity credits.
- eMarket is the market user interface for participation in PJM's day-ahead and regulation markets. Users may submit unit-specific generation offers with operating details, fixed or price-sensitive demand bids, bilateral transactions, and financial increment and decrement bids (Table 7-1).

Wholesale Energy Market	**PJM eMKT / PJM eEES**
FTR Market	**PJM eFTR**
Capacity Credits - Daily **Capacity Credits - Long Term**	**PJM eCapacity**
Regulation	**PJM eMKT**
PJM eSchedules	**Retail Choice Load Balancing**
PJM eGADS	**NERC Generator Availability Data**
PJM eDart	**Facility Outage Scheduling**

Table 7-1 PJM Case Study: Markets and the eSuites

193

Grid accounting

PJM energy market is designed to operate on a balanced basis so that the total amount of charges equals the total amount of credits, leaving no residual funds. Charges and credits for a particular service offset each other exactly. At the end of each operating hour, PJM collects information regarding actual operations during the hour, as recorded by PJM dispatchers or automated systems. Using this information, PJM calculates charges and credits allocated among its members. PJM accounting includes the following services:

- *spot market energy*—energy bought or sold by PJM members through the PJM energy market
- *regulation*—the capability of a specific generating unit to increase or decrease its output in response to a regulating control signal
- *operating reserves*—the amounts of generating capacity scheduled to be available for specified periods of an operating day to ensure reliable operation
- *transmission congestion*—the increased cost of energy delivered when the transmission system is operating under constrained conditions
- *transmission losses*—energy requirements in excess of load requirements attributable to energy consumed by the transmission system's electrical impedance characteristics
- *emergency energy*—energy bought from or sold to another control area by PJM to address emergencies within or outside the PJM control area
- *metering reconciliation*—metering errors and corrections that are reconciled at the end of each month through a meter error correction charge adjustment
- *capacity credit market*—capacity credits bought or sold through the PJM daily and monthly capacity credit markets

Pre-scheduling and scheduling

To fulfill its commitments, PJM establishes and maintains a markets database containing current unit-specific generator information related to operating limits and unit availability for use in pre-scheduling, scheduling, and dispatching. Each generator must advise PJM on a daily basis of its generation schedule and/or bid price for the following day and must abide by the schedule submitted absent permission from PJM to deviate or a *force majeure* event. A generator also must notify PJM whenever station conditions may compel a unit shutdown, whether the restriction is self-imposed or occurs as a result of regulatory action.

To accommodate requirements of the two-settlement system, PJM runs computer programs that perform security-constrained unit commitment and economic dispatch for the day-ahead market based on generation offers, demand bids, increment offers, decrement bids, and transaction schedules submitted by participants, subject to applicable reliability requirements. PJM then calculates hourly unit generation levels and locational marginal prices for all load and generation buses for each hour of the next operating day and creates a powerflow model for each hour of the next operating day based on scheduled network topology, generation and demand profiles, and scheduled tie flow with adjacent areas.

Dispatching of generation

Each generator interconnected with and synchronized to the grid is required to coordinate its operation with PJM by:

- supplying output data and frequency and voltage levels
- scheduling unit operations and outages
- coordinating unit synchronization and disconnection
- providing data required to operate the system and conduct system studies
- providing documented start-up and shutdown procedures, including ramp-up and ramp-down times

- following PJM directions during emergency and restoration conditions
- following PJM-directed operation during transmission-constrained conditions

Generators must maintain black start capability, including voice communication with local control centers via systems tolerant of major power system failure, deliver power in the form of 3-phase, 60-Hertz alternating current at the nominal system voltage at the point of interconnection and operating at specified frequencies to accommodate under-frequency load shedding, and respond immediately to a PJM request directing a change in output until the prescribed load is reached. Generators also must operate units according to a predefined voltage schedule or a reactive power schedule provided by PJM.

Under emergency conditions PJM has the authority to direct deviation from pre-scheduled values in accordance with applicable reliability principles. Generators are expected to take all requested actions to manage, alleviate, or end an emergency. The local control center may direct a generator to increase or decrease energy and/or reactive output, connect or disconnect a unit from the PJM system, and/or deviate from the prescribed voltage or reactive schedules (Table 7-2). Generators are also subject to specific switching, relaying, training, maintenance, and reporting requirements.

Criteria for determining certain emergency conditions are reviewed in the following table:

Condition	Alert	Warning	Initiation
Maximum Emergency Generation	Requested in Operating Plan on prior day.		When demand is greater than highest normal bid.
Primary Reserve	Reserve is less than primary requirement.	Reserve is less than primary requirement but greater than spinning reserve.	
Load Management Curtailment			When generation is not available to meet forecast demand.
Voltage Reduction	Estimated reserve is less than forecast spinning reserve requirement.	Spinning reserve less than spinning requirement.	When load relief is needed to maintain tie schedules or relieve transmission constraints.
Voluntary Customer Load Curtailment	Forecasted reserve indicates a probable need this action.		When earlier procedures have not produced needed load relief.
Radio / TV Appeal			When earlier procedures have not produced needed load relief.
Manual Load Dump		Reserves are less than largest contingency.	When earlier procedures have not produced needed load relief.

Table 7–2 Criteria for Determining Certain Emergency Conditions

Data and communication requirements

PJM's lifeblood is information, and it has established an energy management system (EMS) through which data is exchanged with member companies via dedicated redundant data circuits. [4] EMS data transmitted by members to PJM includes data needed for PJM control programs and for monitoring generation, transmission, and interchange. EMS data transmitted by PJM to members includes system control data, generation, and transmission information required for monitoring and security analysis programs, area regulation data, and reserve data.

The PJM supervisory control and data acquisition (SCADA) system allows PJM to communicate directly with individual generators or smaller control centers using computer, database and digital communications technology.[5] The SCADA system allows transfer of both generation and revenue data and real-time bi-directional transfer of analog and digital data for storage and transfer. All customers connecting to PJM in real-time must be able to support a minimum data model. Other communication options include a combination of electronic data, dispatch and business voice links, facsimile, Internet communications, and materials sent by courier or mail.

To model, schedule, and monitor the PJM system, each generator is required to submit data (*e.g.*, MW, MVAR, MWh, bus voltages, circuit breaker status, 3-phase amperage, etc.) automatically with respect to power system applications, production cost and reliability assessment, including:

- expected unit operations and desired market service/segment
- stability study data
- step-up transformer data
- relay settings and generator protection package
- generator operating curves and associated test data
- special operating restrictions
- identification of equipment ownership and maintenance responsibilities
- test data for metering calibration, backup communications, and relays

PJM does not require direct connection. Generators can instead negotiate data transmission to and from PJM through the local utility or transmission facilities owner, supplemented by the use of Internet-based eSchedules and eData.

Notes

[1] If the ISA has been executed, PJM files it with FERC in accordance with applicable guidelines. If the applicant requests dispute resolution or makes an unexecuted filing, construction of facilities and upgrades is deferred until disputes are resolved

[2] PJM offers expedited procedures for interconnection of new resources of less than 10 MW or increases of less than 10 MW to existing generation

[3] The unforced capacity rating of a unit is defined as the installed capacity multiplied by (1-EFORd). A unit with an installed capacity rating of 100 MW and EFORd of 10% would have (1-EFORd) equal to .9, resulting in an unforced rating of 100 MW multiplied by .9, or 90 MW

[4] PJM is in transition to the Inter-control Center Communications Protocol, a comprehensive international standard for real-time data exchange

[5] PJM*net* is a new, redundant network that PJM is installing as the primary wide-area network for communicating control center voice and data to and from PJM. PJM*net* will support Inter-Control Center Communications Protocol data links to control centers—SCADA links to plants via remote terminal units and generator all-call to control centers

CHAPTER EIGHT

Governance and Management

Governance issues have shaped PJM's development and operations from its inception as an ISO. PJM's governance adheres to FERC's cardinal principle that an ISO's decision-making process be "independent of control by any market participant or class of participants."[1] To achieve independence, PJM relies on a two-tiered structure that includes a fully independent non-stakeholder board of governors (the PJM board), elected to staggered terms by two-thirds majority vote, and a sectoral members committee to provide advisory support. For voting purposes, each member is assigned to one of five sectors: generation owners, other suppliers, transmission owners, electric distributors, and end-use customers. Any entity that owns transmission facilities in the PJM control area or is an "eligible customer" as defined in the PJM tariff can become a member of PJM.

The structure provides a forum for collaborative solutions but does not compromise the PJM board's independence. In the words of Phillip G. Harris, PJM's president, "The decision made in 1992 to separate PJM from the administrative oversight of a single member and to establish . . . governance that would be neutral to all members, was a precursor to PJM's roles as the nation's premier independent system operator and has proven to be a key positive decision in meeting the electric needs of the Mid-Atlantic region."[2]

Overview

As an institution, PJM is independent of market participants. Neither PJM, its employees, nor its non-stakeholder directors owns stock or has any other financial interest, direct or indirect, in any market participant.[3] Equally, PJM does not take title to any energy in any of the markets it operates. Nor does PJM own any generation resources or transmission facilities. At the same time, PJM is a limited liability company whose members include transmission owners and other market participants.[4]

Under its Operating Agreement, PJM's members have certain ownership and voting rights, including the right to return of capital contributed and liquidating distributions.[5] Through the members committee, PJM's members also elect (but do not select or nominate) the PJM board,[6] retain advisory prerogatives, and have the power to terminate the Operating Agreement subject to FERC's approval.[7] Notwithstanding those powers, PJM's members are precluded from "[taking] part in the management of [its] business . . ."[8] PJM's governance reflects a structural compromise to accommodate the transmission owners' initial desire to preserve residual oversight and management's need to operate independently.

PJM's operational success is more than a product of its institutional structure. It is also, significantly, attributable to Phil Harris' vision, political astuteness, and managerial skill.[9] In presiding over PJM's transition from administrative adjunct to fully functioning RTO, Harris has adroitly balanced the interests of diverse constituencies, often at odds with each other, to produce a largely seamless result. Through a collaborative stakeholder process,

Harris has caused PJM to implement effective market rules, timely distribution of useful information, and tools that enable participants to take effective action benefiting themselves and the market at the same time.

In doing so, Harris has responded to and interpreted certain industry-wide trends:

- Decision-making within PJM is not exclusively an internal process. It has been rendered transparent and accessible to market participants, who are actively engaged in determining the services PJM provides. To serve its marketplace, PJM has built long-term relationships with its members, worked collaboratively, and sought feedback wherever possible

- To meet participants' expectations, PJM has consistently provided as many choices as possible, based in part on member-designed solutions to perceived problems

- PJM has also offered Internet applications that facilitate real-time information access and market readiness. PJM provides multiple choices in the hourly and next day energy markets and supports five specialty markets as well. With independent administration of the hourly market, members can establish exchanges to coordinate physical deliveries. In the day-ahead market members can submit bids to buy or sell energy or both, based on generation and expected load or upon pure speculation. Members can also arrange bilateral transactions with other parties and jointly confirm those transactions through the Internet, creating schedules that adjust their interchanges automatically. In hourly markets, members owning resources can self-schedule and participate to support other arrangements or for strategic reasons

- PJM has addressed rapid change in the restructured electric industry by encouraging the very innovations and adaptations it is then called upon to manage, thus transforming the industrial environment in which it operates. Examples include PJM's locational marginal price model and Internet tools for state retail programs

- PJM has customized and adapted its solutions to serve stakeholders with diverse and exponentially expanding needs

PJM's two-tiered governance model, coupled with member participation in decision-making, provides a forum for debate and participation. When PJM's business rules require adaptation to market conditions, change occurs fairly, collaboratively, and efficiently. As evidence, PJM can point to more than 80 successful modifications of the PJM tariff and constituent agreements since it became an ISO in 1997. PJM also continues to involve stakeholders through its public processes and committee structure, both of which reflect Harris' pragmatic, innovative, and technically driven management style.

PJM board

The PJM board, whose express responsibility is to maintain reliability, create robust and competitive markets, and prevent undue influence by any member or group of members, manages PJM.[10] The members of the PJM board have agreed not to take part in the management of or transact business for PJM in their capacity as members and have no power to sign for or legally bind PJM.[11] The PJM board acts by majority vote if a quorum is present (a majority of the full board constituting a quorum), but certain actions require a 70% super-majority, including removal of a board member, merger or consolidation, disposition of PJM's assets, and conversion or division of PJM. Those actions also require an amendment to the Operating Agreement and FERC approval.[12]

The PJM board is a non-stakeholder board that meets FERC's independence criterion. The members committee elects it from a slate of candidates prepared by an independent consultant, not by the PJM members.[13] Of the seven outside PJM board members (PJM's president being an eighth *ex officio* member), four are required to have expertise and experience in corporate leadership at the senior management or board level or in the professional disciplines of finance or accounting, engineering, or utility laws or regulation. Of the remaining three PJM board members, one must have expertise and experience in the operation of transmission dependent utilities, one in operation or planning of transmission systems, and one in commercial markets, trading and associated risk management.[14]

PJM board members have no affiliations with PJM members. Under the Operating Agreement, the PJM board must perform its duties and responsibilities consistent with the principle that no member or group of members may have undue influence over PJM's operations.[15] A PJM board member "shall not be, and shall not have been at any time within five years of election to the PJM Board a director, officer or employee of a [PJM] Member or of an Affiliate or Related Party of a Member."[16] The Operating Agreement also requires that "[e]xcept as provided in [PJM's] Standards of Conduct filed with the FERC, at any time while serving on the PJM Board, a Board Member shall have no direct business relationship or other affiliation with any Member or its Affiliates or Related Parties."[17] To reinforce these measures of independence, as noted, the Operating Agreement requires that PJM members may not participate in the management of or act for PJM.[18] The PJM board can thus fairly be said to represent the public interest.

In addition to its broad-based policy concerns, noted above, the PJM board is charged with responsibility for supervising all matters pertaining to PJM and its operations, including (upon consideration of the recommendations of the finance committee) approval of operating and capital budgets.[19] Among other powers, the PJM board also:

- selects PJM's officers
- approves the regional transmission expansion plan
- submits to the members committee proposed changes in the Operating Agreement
- petitions FERC to modify any provision of the Operating Agreement it believes to be unjust, unreasonable or unduly discriminatory under Section 206 of the Federal Power Act
- intervenes in FERC proceedings initiated by members and participates in other state and federal regulatory proceedings relating to PJM's interests
- establishes sanctions for a member's failure to comply with its obligations under the Operating Agreement
- directs PJM to take appropriate legal or regulatory action against a member to recover any unpaid amounts due under the Operating Agreement and "as may otherwise be necessary to enforce obligations under the Operating Agreement"

- resolves members' claims that the reliability committee established under the Reliability Assurance Agreement has not acted consistently with creation and operation of a robust, competitive, and non-discriminatory electric power market in the PJM control area
- solicits members' views on, and obtains independent reviews of performance of, the PJM interchange energy market, market participants' compliance with market rules and requirements, and PJM's performance under criteria proposed by the members committee and approved by the PJM board

PJM's non-stakeholder board is essential to PJM's governance and has acquired its present broad powers following sequential negotiations with transmission owners and other market participants concerned to protect their assets and interests from unilateral decision-making. A critical issue, resolved in favor of the PJM board, is its ability to amend the PJM tariff. Under Order No. 2000's mandate, an RTO "must have the independent and exclusive right to make Section 205 filings that apply to the rates, terms and conditions of transmission service over the facilities operated by the RTO."[20]

Even before issuing Order No. 2000, however, FERC had determined that "PJM may file a proposed amendment to the PJM [tariff] without obtaining the Member Committee's prior approval."[21] The role of the members committee is therefore advisory. It may recommend or endorse tariff changes but has no power to prohibit them. At the same time, under Order No. 2000-A, transmission owners have the right independently to make filings pursuant to Section 205 "to establish their revenue requirements and the just and reasonable payments they may charge the RTO for use of their facilities."[22] Accordingly, the Transmission Owners Agreement provides that "[e]ach Party shall have the right at any time unilaterally to file pursuant to Section 205 of the Federal Power Act to change the revenue requirements underlying its rates for providing services under the PJM tariff."[23] Nonetheless, because the transmission owners cannot make Section 205 filings to change the terms and conditions of PJM's services to customers, their ability to change their revenue requirements does not interfere with PJM's independence.[24]

Through its two-tier governance structure, PJM has also avoided two other potential pitfalls confronted by an independent non-stakeholder board—lack of sufficient feedback from stakeholders and dilatory decision-making when confronted with difficult issues. Although stakeholder committees are subordinate to the PJM board, they remain collaboratively involved. The PJM board has the requisite knowledge to evaluate and act disinterestedly on information received. The success of PJM's governance system rests on the PJM board's independence, its mix of relevant skills and experience, the broadly representative nature of the members committee, maintenance of formal and informal channels of communication between the PJM board and stakeholders, and the continuing obligation of the PJM board to assess whether applicable rules and procedures are consistent with fair and efficient operation, *i.e.,* to exercise oversight based on a public interest standard rather than to advance the interests of a particular group or class of stakeholders.[25]

In these respects, the PJM board is different from a typical corporate board, which is required to pursue maximization of shareholder value. Unlike corporate shareholders, PJM's members and market participants represent widely divergent and conflicting economic interests, often directly in competition with each other for generation sales and customers. By remaining independent of PJM's members, the PJM board preserves its neutrality and integrity as a governing body.

Members Committee

The Members Committee enjoys limited and balanced powers. As noted, it may elect the PJM board from a slate of candidates selected by an independent consultant, form additional advisory committees, amend and terminate the Operating Agreement (subject to FERC approval), and advise the PJM board.[26] The members committee conducts its business by sector vote, and includes generation owners, other suppliers, transmission owners, electric distributors, and end-use customers.[27] Members may be active in only one sector at a time, and only one affiliate of a related corporate group may be active in a selected sector.[28]

Each sector must have at least five members, and each has one vote that is divided into positive and negative components in direct proportion to the votes of the sector members for a particular motion.[29] To pass a pending motion, the sum of the affirmative votes must be greater than the product of .667 multiplied by the number of sectors that have at least five members and have participated in the vote.[30] Accordingly, the members committee cannot act, even in its advisory role, without approval of a two-thirds majority of the sectors.

The members committee may form, select the membership, and oversee the activities of an operating committee (operating principles, practices, and procedures), a planning committee (planning principles, practices, and procedures), and an energy market committee. Other major committees include a tariff advisory committee, reliability assurance committee, audit advisory committee, alternative dispute resolution committee, and finance committee. Members sharing a common interest may also form users groups, and the members committee is required to create a users group composed of representatives of *bona fide* public interest and environmental organizations interested in PJM's activities.[31]

Members

To qualify as a member of PJM, an entity must:

- be a transmission owner within the PJM control area or an eligible customer under the PJM tariff
- if not a transmission owner, be a generation owner, other supplier, electric distributor, or end-use customer
- be engaged in buying, selling, or transmitting electric energy in or through PJM or intend to do so
- accept its obligations under the Operating Agreement[32]

Load-serving entities that become members must also become parties to the Reliability Assurance Agreement.[33] Electric distributor members must comply with PJM's standards for system design, equipment ratings, operations, and maintenance practices. Such members must also have energy management systems compatible with PJM's, employ automatic load-shedding devices, provide reactive capability and voltage control facilities, initiate active load management programs, maintain capacity resources capable of start-up without assistance from the grid, and maintain local control centers to coordinate with PJM through telemetry and system operators.[34]

Members are required to make full and timely payment of all charges arising under the Operating Agreement or the PJM tariff. A defaulting member is precluded from buying or selling energy in the PJM interchange energy market, voting, and participating in committee activities.[35] Members also indemnify each other against certain liabilities and are required to make specific representations and warranties in the Operating Agreement.[36]

As noted, members are expressly precluded from taking part in PJM's management, transacting business for PJM, or signing for or legally binding PJM.[37] At the same time, members are required as applicable to engage in coordinated planning and system operations within the PJM control area. This reflects a degree of interactive cooperation that has proved to be the hallmark of PJM's growth and organizational success. PJM presently has more than 180 members, most of whom are active market participants. The ever-increasing volume of transactions in PJM's markets is evidence that its governance structure facilitates commerce. In 1999 PJM administered $1.8 billion in market transactions, including spot market energy, capacity market transactions, ancillary services, and transmission services. During the same period PJM responded to 350 million MW hours of transmission service requests and more than 120 million MW hours of scheduled energy transactions.

Officers

Under the Operating Agreement, PJM's officers include a President, Secretary, Treasurer and "such other officers as [are] necessary to carry out [PJM's] business . . . ,"[38] all of whom are elected by the PJM board. The President directs PJM's functions as set forth in the Operating Agreement. Among the most important of these are:

- directing operation of PJM's facilities used for both load and reactive supply to maintain reliability and obtain the benefits of pooling and interchange
- directing operation of PJM's bulk power supply facilities
- directing operation of PJM's transmission facilities, administering the PJM tariff, administering the RTEP protocol, and performing transferred responsibilities under the Reliability Assurance Agreement
- performing emergency monitoring, planning and management functions
- initiating legal and regulatory proceedings as directed by the PJM board[39]

PJM's governance structure accords the president plenary operational responsibility, subject to oversight of the PJM board. This division of responsibility is critical to efficient operations since the PJM board cannot be expected to address the manifold details of PJM's day-to-day operations. At the same time, under Phil Harris' direction, the PJM presidency has moved beyond command-and-control concepts to reflect managerial best practices based on recent experience.

In a networked and information-based industry, the locus of decision-making within PJM is shifting from internal corporate mechanisms to external participants. Business processes are publicly available, and members actively determine the services to be provided. PJM posts real-time energy market prices on public Internet pages every five minutes for approximately 150 hubs, zones, and significant locations throughout the PJM control area. It similarly posts emergency procedures within minutes of their declaration to facilitate market support during emergency conditions.

PJM has also implemented the nation's first FERC-approved transmission expansion plan to enable new resources to enter competitive markets. In these and other ways PJM provides choices, leading to collaboratively designed and customized solutions. PJM has also had the wisdom to implement markets sequentially, thereby benefiting from prior experience and protecting service already in existence. PJM thus combines reliability requirements and sophisticated market rules under independent administration to support diversity, market maturity, and growth.

Financial independence

PJM has exclusive and independent control over recovery of its own costs through the PJM tariff and as a result is financially self-sufficient.[40] Tariff-based cost recovery has permitted PJM to acquire, from the transmission owners, ownership of information technology and other capital assets previously used by it, and essential to its functions as an ISO.

As noted, PJM is the successor to PJM Interconnection Association (PJMIA), an unincorporated association formed by several member utilities to administer a tight power pool. PJMIA operated the PJM control center and service center in Pennsylvania under agreements whereby the member utilities owned, as tenants in common, the "land, structures, and fixtures" comprising PJMIA's control center and service center, "together with suitable furnishings and equipment" based on stated ownership percentages. PJMIA in practice made all capital spending decisions, and the transmission owners paid all capital billings.

When PJM became an ISO in 1997, the transmission owners not only owned transmission lines, transformers, and other electrical system equipment but also the PJM office complex, including the control center, the service center, furniture, equipment, and computer hardware and software. PJM had no property rights in those assets. Instead PJM and the transmission owners continued to operate under pre-existing arrangements whereby PJM determined which capital assets it required and then billed each of the transmission owners a predetermined share of PJM's expenditures for those capital assets.

In keeping with FERC's central focus on ISO independence, however, PJM recognized the importance of having clearly defined property rights. In 1998 PJM commenced arm's-length negotiations with the transmission owners to acquire ownership of the subject assets, including:

- its energy management system, which allows PJM to monitor and control the generation and transmission system
- the PJM OASIS
- accounting and billing systems for transmission service, ancillary services, the energy market, and other services
- information systems to facilitate retail choice

- enhancements to the PJM back-up control center
- customizable Internet publication of system data and on-line energy scheduling capabilities
- the FTR auction
- other related systems

PJM's negotiations with the transmission owners culminated in an agreement dated December 29, 1999 calling for the transmission owners to lease PJM the real property, buildings, improvements, and fixtures at the PJM control center and service center, sell PJM certain identified assets, and assign to PJM certain identified intellectual property rights, licenses, and trademarks. The lease runs for 25 years at a nominal rent. The intellectual property rights assigned included patents, copyrights, know-how, trade secrets, licensed intellectual property, and licensed trademarks.

For the assets acquired as purchaser and assignee, PJM agreed to pay each transmission owner a purchase price equal to the transmission owner's "book cost," the cost to the transmission owner of income taxes attributable to the equity portion of allowance for funds used during construction (AFUDC) included in its "book cost," funds provided by the transmission owner to PJM after January 1, 2000 but before closing, and applicable interest from January 1, 2000 through closing. As of December 31, 1999 the transmission owners' aggregate "book cost" was $103.7 million, subject to an equity AFUDC income tax addition of $3.3 million.

PJM thereafter revised the PJM tariff to unbundle the PJM cost recovery charge by means of new Schedule 9 containing several separate service categories, each including a formula rate for recovery of the costs thereof.[41] It also asked FERC to find the purchase price for the subject assets to be just and reasonable and permit PJM to recover its acquisition costs under the PJM tariff[42] since PJM's obligation to close the asset acquisition was conditioned upon express assurance that the costs of acquisition would be fully recoverable under the PJM tariff, a matter of singular concern to PJM's lenders. Recovery was also viewed as an important question of policy since it would permit PJM, upon purchasing the assets from the transmission owners, to pursue independent development and would be consistent with FERC's encouragement of fully functioning, independent RTOs.

PJM noted that the price under the acquisition agreement equaled no more than the original cost of amounts paid over time by the transmission owners to PJM, plus reasonable carrying charges, and that none of those costs had been included in the transmission owners' rates for service to their customers. PJM justified acquisition of the subject assets as a means of "[eliminating] any perception of a threat to its independence . . . and [making] a clean transition to self-funding of its capital requirements."[43] PJM also noted that asset transfer would allow it to leverage its expertise by marketing its systems to other RTOs and offsetting PJM expenses with the resulting revenues.[44]

To meet its purchase obligations and close the acquisition on December 1, 2000, PJM sought FERC authorization under Section 204 of the Federal Power Act to raise as much as $191 million through a private bond placement or a secured loan.

Market monitoring

An ISO such as PJM, with broad powers to operate the grid and manage a power exchange, is also a logical vehicle to curb market abuses. With FERC-approved open access transmission tariffs as a platform, ISOs can in principle implement market monitoring to acquire detailed market information, intervene, if necessary, to prevent market power abuse, and even employ sanctions to prevent strategic withholding of capacity and use of transmission constraints to exclude competitors.

In its November 25, 1997 order approving PJM as an ISO, FERC required that it adopt a monitoring plan addressing "the potential to exercise market power within [the PJM power pool]," including an evaluation of both pool and bilateral markets and "any proposed enforcement mechanisms that are necessary to assure compliance with pool rules."[45] In doing so, FERC was mindful of a concern expressed by consultants for the PJM companies that "[t]hose who own . . . specific generators . . . that must be run for reliability purposes could, if unconstrained by contract or regulation, extract monopoly profits. The owners of such must-run generation could bid very high prices for their output, and the ISO would be forced to call on them to operate for reliability reasons even if the energy which they provide could be replaced by cheaper sources absent the must-run constraints."[46]

FERC's regulations require an RTO to "provide for objective monitoring of markets it operates or administers to identify market design flaws, market power abuses and opportunities for efficiency improvement, and [to] propose appropriate actions."[47] Such monitoring must address:

- the behavior of market participants, including transmission owners, to determine if their actions impair the RTO's capability to provide reliable, efficient, and non-discriminatory transmission service
- how behavior in markets operated by others (*e.g.*, bilateral power sales markets and power markets operated by unaffiliated power exchanges) affects RTO operations and, reciprocally, how RTO operations affect the efficiency of power markets operated by others
- the filing of reports to FERC and other regulatory authorities concerning opportunities for efficiency improvement, market power abuses, and market design flaws[48]

In Order No. 2000 FERC provided further guidance as to RTO market monitoring plans, which must:

- identify the specific markets to be monitored
- examine the structure of each subject market, compliance with market rules, behavior of individual market participants, market power, and market abuses
- address how information is to be used and reported
- indicate whether the RTO will merely identify problems and abuses or whether it will also propose solutions
- identify any proposed sanctions or penalties and the specific conduct subject thereto
- provide a rationale to support sanctions, penalties, or remedies and explain how they are to be implemented
- indicate the type and frequency of reports to be made and the recipients thereof
- provide an objective basis for observing and analyzing markets
- limit information to that gathered in the ordinary course of business

Given these requirements, it is indispensable that an RTO be independent of market participants in order to monitor market power effectively and disinterestedly. An appropriate governance structure, such as PJM's, is essential for this purpose.

PJM had implemented a conforming market monitoring plan (MMP) prior to issuance of Order No. 2000[49] and had established a market monitoring unit (MMU) within PJM to "independently and objectively monitor and report on the operation of the PJM Market."[50] The MMU's monitoring responsibilities include matters relating to transmission congestion pricing, exercise of market power, structural problems in the PJM market, design flaws in the operating rules, and compliance with the standards, procedures, and practices in the PJM tariff, Operating Agreement, Reliability Assurance Agreement and PJM manuals.[51] The MMU also has authority to recommend to the PJM board or to FERC modifications to PJM's rules, standards, and practices.[52]

The MMU also has enforcement authority and, by means of a demand letter, may request that a market participant discontinue actions that violate the PJM tariff, other PJM agreements, or applicable market rules and procedures.[53] If the demand letter or informal discussions do not suffice, the MMU may refer the matter to the members committee or the PJM board; with the approval of the PJM board, file reports or complaints with FERC or other regulatory authorities to address design flaws, structural problems or compliance, or request remedial action; and may consider additional enforcement mechanisms to assure compliance.[54] However, the MMU itself does not have sanctioning authority.[55]

The MMU is required to submit a detailed public report annually and issued the first such report in July 2000. It also submits periodic reports concerning the state of competition within and efficiency of the PJM market to the PJM board, the members committee, FERC and other government agencies, including recommendations as to any changes required in the MMP itself.[56] In its initial annual report the MMU recommended rule changes for the PJM capacity markets, including a market-based mechanism to give load-serving entities an incentive to deliver energy from capacity resources to loads at a level consistent with the claimed capacity of generation units, a requirement that load-serving entities meet their capacity obligations on an annual or semiannual basis, and a requirement that capacity resources be offered on an annual or semiannual basis with a bid cap.[57] The MMU is also required to develop and refine indices or other standards for the purpose of objectively evaluating the behavior of market participants.[58]

Market monitoring encompasses data such as available transmission capacity calculations, transmission reserve margins, capacity benefit margins, and projected load and system contingencies. FERC is also seeking to expand the scope of reported information to include transaction data (number of transactions, amount of each transaction in MW, and all connected paths from point of receipt to point of delivery), curtailment data, real-time condition of the transmission network, including transmission and generation outages, and load, generation, and tie-line flow data in each control area.

PJM Technologies, Inc.

Having agreed with the transmission owners to acquire from them information systems, intellectual property, and related assets, PJM properly viewed itself as an information company—not just a regulated utility but the owner of valuable proprietary expertise, methodologies, and databases. The proliferation of ISOs and prospective RTOs, under FERC's regulatory guidance, has provided a ready domestic market for PJM's know-how. PJM's successful formula of Internet technology and innovative market rules is also sought by power systems throughout the world. PJM has thus recognized substantial commercial prospects for such technology as:

- *Energy Management System*—integrates transmission outage scheduling, monitoring and control functions
- *Energy Market Pricing System*—allows PJM to determine the locational marginal price for load and generator buses of the PJM system
- *Two-Settlement System*—allows PJM to develop day-ahead hourly supply and demand schedules and hourly energy prices based on bid prices and quantities

In September 2000 PJM organized a for-profit, wholly owned subsidiary, PJM Technologies, Inc. (PJM Tech), to undertake commercial development of its intellectual property assets. PJM granted PJM Tech a non-exclusive, worldwide, non-transferable license to its intellectual property coupled with a right permitting PJM Tech to enter into sublicenses with third parties. PJM Tech anticipates figuring prominently in PJM initiatives with respect to other ISOs and its collaboration with RTE, the French transmission system operator, with which PJM has agreed to share technical knowledge and information.

Notes

[1] *Order No. 2000,* FERC, ¶ 31,089, p. 31,061

[2] *Testimony of Phillip G. Harris, President and Chief Executive Officer of PJM, before the Maryland Public Service Commission,* October 23, 2000; mimeo, p. 2

[3] See *FERC Regulations* at 18 C.F.R. § 35.34 (j)(1)(i)(2000)

[4] PJM presently has more than 200 members, including 10 transmission owners, 70 load aggregators, more than 100 traders and 2,000 OASIS users

[5] *Operating Agreement,* §§ 6.2 and 6.3. Section 6.2(b) states that PJM "does not intend to make any distributions of cash or other assets to its members"

[6] Id. at § 7.1

[7] Id. at §§ 8.8 and 4.1(c)

[8] Id. at § 11.1

[9] A 25-year energy industry veteran, Harris has served in executive positions in generation, transmission and finance, culminating in the presidency of PJM Interconnection, LLC. He is a Certified Management Accountant and a Certified Computer Systems Professional, has served on the boards of directors of the Southwest Power Pool and the Southwest Resource Association, is a member of the North American Reliability Council Board of Trustees, and serves as Regional Manager of the Mid-Atlantic Area Council. He is a member of the National Association of Corporate Directors. Harris frequently provides expert testimony on electric restructuring issues and has appeared before many federal and state commissions and legislatures. He has authored articles about the competitive electric market place and has been featured as subject matter expert by the media, including the *Wall Street Journal, Forbes,* and *Fortune.* Harris has also forged partnerships between PJM and Electricate de France and Tokyo Electric Power Company, operators of the world's largest and second largest power grids, respectively. Harris is a graduate of the United States Military Academy and holds an M.B.A. from the University of Northern Colorado with emphasis on Research and Statistical Methodology

[10] *Operating Agreement* § 7.7(i)

[11] Id. § 11.1

[12] Id. § 18.6(c)

[13] Incumbent members of the PJM Board include Carolyn S. Burger, former president and CEO, Bell Atlantic Delaware, Inc.; John T. Coughlin, former Commissioner, Wisconsin Public Service Commission; Lynn W. Eury, former Director and Executive Vice President, Carolina Power and Light Company; Phillip G. Harris, President and CEO, PJM Interconnection, L.L.C.; James E. Ksansnak, Vice Chairman and Director, ARAMARK Corporation; Dr. Richard T. Lahey, Jr., Edward E. Hook Professor of

Engineering and former Dean, Rensselaer Polytechnic Institute; Frank L. Olson, President and General Manager and board member, Municipal Electric Authority of Georgia, and Howard Schneider, Esq., Senior Partner, Rosenman & Colin L.L.P., and former General Counsel, Commodity Futures Trading Commission.

[14] Id. § 7.2.

[15] Id. § 7.7(i)

[16] Id. § 7.2

[17] Id. §7.2 PJM's Standards of Conduct permit PJM board members to indirectly own securities issued by a PJM member, customer or market participant through a mutual fund or similar arrangement under which the PJM board member does not control the purchase or sale of such securities. *FERC Order No. 889 Standards of Conduct* § B.4, submitted by PJM in Docket Nol. ER97-3189-011 on December 31, 1997. Under the Standards of Conduct, "officers and employees of PJM shall not have a direct financial interest in, or stand to be financially benefitted by, any transaction with any Member, Eligible Customer or Market Participant." The Standards of Conduct also provide for a six-month period from the time of affiliation with PJM for all employees, officers and PJM board members to divest any securities that violate this rule. There is also a six-month period within which to divest such securities if a PJM board member, officer, or employee receives the same by gift or if such person owns any securities in an entity that becomes a new member, customer or market participant. Id. §§ B.1, B.12, B.3. This divestiture plan follows FERC's directives in the PJM ISO Order to ensure financial independence and is consistent with Order No. 888. See *PJM ISO Order*, 81 FERC at 62,266; Order No. 888 at 31,731

[18] Id. at § 11.1

[19] Id., § 7.5.2

[20] *Order No. 2000*, at 31,075; see also 18 C.F.R. § 35.34(j)(1)(iii)

[21] *PJM Interconnection, L.L.C.*, 86 FERC ¶ 61,247, at 61,890 (1999). On several occasions, the PJM board has acted independently of the members committee and has made filings with FERC to amend the PJM tariff and the Operating Agreement even when such action has not been supported by a two-thirds sector majority of the members committee. See, *e.g., PJM Interconnection, L.L.C.*, 89 FERC ¶ 61,281 (1999); *PJM Interconnection, L.L.C.*, 92 FERC ¶ 61,013 (2000)

[22] *Order No. 2000-A*, at 31,270

[23] *Transmission Owners Agreement*, § 2.2.1

[24] *Order No. 2000*, at 31,976

[25] See Barker, Tenenbaum, and Woolf, *Governance and Regulation of Power Pools and System Operators*, World Bank Technical Paper No. 382 (1997), pp. 11-12

[26] *Operating Agreement*, §§ 8.6, 8.8

[27] Id., § 8.1.1

[28] Id., §§ 8.1.1 and 8.1.2

[29] Id., § 8.4(b)

[30] Id., § 8.4(c)

[31] Id., § 8.7(b)

[32] Id., § 11.6(a)

[33] Id., § 11.6(b)

[34] Id., § 11.3.3

[35] Id., § 15.1.3

[36] Id., §§ 16.1 and 17.1

[37] Id., § 11.1. Members nonetheless retain rights to petition FERC under Sections 205 and 206 of the Federal Power Act. *Id.,* § 11.5

[38] Id., § 9.1

[39] Id., § 10.4

[40] PJM collects its costs through a series of unbundled charges as set forth in Schedule 9 to the PJM tariff. See *PJM Interconnection, L.L.C.,* 92 FERC ¶ 61,114 (2000)

[41] FERC Docket No. ER00-298-000

[42] See *PJM Interconnection, L.L.C., Petition for Declaratory Order* filed in FERC Docket No. EL-95-000

[43] Id. *Cf. New England Power Pool,* 79 FERC ¶ 61,374, at 62,590 (1997)

[44] See discussion below with respect to PJM Technologies, Inc.

[45] *Pennsylvania-New Jersey-Maryland Interconnection,* 81 FERC ¶ 61,257 (1997)

[46] *Supporting Companies' Report on Horizontal Market Power Analysis* dated July 14, 1997, FERC Docket Nos. OA97-261-000 and ER97-1082-000

[47] 18 C.F.R. §35.34(k)(6)(2000)

[48] Id., § 35.34(k)(6)(i)-(iii)(2000)

[49] See *PJM Interconnection L.L.C.,* 86 FERC ¶ 61,247 (1999)

[50] Id. at 61,887; see also *PJM tariff,* Attachment M § I (Objectives)

[51] Id.

[52] *PJM tariff,* Attachment M § IV.A.2

[53] Id. § IV.A. 3

[54] Id. § IV. A. 3-6

[55] See Lambert, "ISOs as Market Regulators: The Emerging Debate," *Public Utilities Fortnightly,* April 15, 1998. The prospect that ISOs could impose sanctions and penalties gave rise to strong objections from transmission owners and others

[56] *PJM tariff,* Attachment M §§ VII.A-C

[57] *PJM Interconnection State of the Market Report 1999,* PJM Market Monitoring Unit, June 2000, p. 8

[58] Id. § VI.E. See *Order No. 2000* at 31,156

CHAPTER NINE 9

Epilogue

In a few short years PJM has undergone a remarkable transformation. Initially an administrative adjunct to a regulated tight power pool, PJM is now a major system operator, market maker, and technological innovator. PJM's transition to competition has turned on four underlying decisions:

- PJM has built an established regional base in a multi-state area, providing a large number and diversity of market participants resulting in a highly liquid market (Fig. 9-1)
- PJM has combined the spot market with real-time dispatch. Linking the dispatcher's actions to the spot prices bid into the markets has harmonized bid prices and physical dispatch

- PJM implemented regional planning prior to commencement of a competitive energy market, enabling all participants to understand and work through a common process for modifying and installing new capacity in a five-state region
- PJM has used an incremental approach to instituting the many changes required in so massive an undertaking. PJM makes incremental changes, monitors and evaluates them, and collaborates with all parties in assessing their effectiveness. Incrementalism reduces the risk of missteps in design and operation of the multi-billion industry under PJM's control

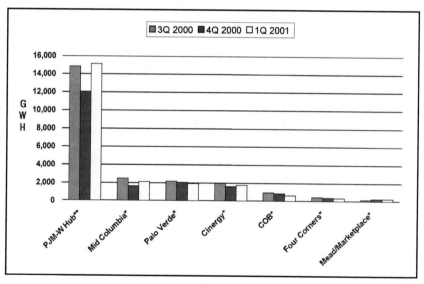

Fig. 9–1 Market Liquidity

PJM has successfully realized the theoretical projection made almost 20 years ago. PJM makes scheduling, re-dispatch, and maintenance decisions independent of its members' commercial interests, is the sole administrator of its open access tariff, has implemented a queue system to deal with generation interconnection, and has clear authority to direct transmission owners to construct upgrades or additional facilities as necessary. PJM's reliance on locational marginal pricing eliminates any requirement to negotiate and manage re-dispatch with its generator members on a bilateral basis.

PJM also administers both a spot market and bilateral schedules, maintains reliability through economic dispatch, offers a balancing service, and has implemented a system of tradable fixed transmission rights as a means of hedging congestion costs. PJM thus promotes the long-run competitiveness of the marketplace but does not seek to maximize either its own profitability as RTO or that of any market participant. PJM also has primary responsibility for transmission planning in the PJM control area and is free to solve transmission constraints by building additional transmission or interconnecting new generation. In performing these functions, PJM has emerged as the clear industry leader, a paradigm for the management and development of competitive markets in electric power.

INDEX

L

M

R

S

T

U

W

Other titles offered by PennWell...

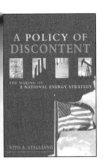

A Policy of Discontent: The Making of a National Energy Strategy
by Vito A. Stagliano
446 pages, hardcover
$39.95 US/CAN
$54.95 Intl
ISBN: 0-87814-817-5

Managing Energy Risk: A Nontechnical Guide to Markets and Trading
by John Wengler
393 pages, hardcover
$64.95 US/CAN
$79.95 Intl
ISBN: 0-87814-794-2

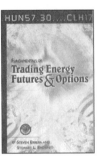

Fundamentals of Trading Energy Futures & Options
by Steven Errera and Stewart Brown
253 pages, hardcover
$64.95 US/CAN
$79.95 Intl
ISBN: 0-87814-760-8

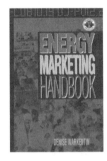

Energy Marketing Handbook
by Denise Warkentin
197 pages, hardcover
$64.95 US/CAN
$79.95 Intl
ISBN: 0-87814-604-0

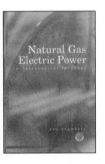

Natural Gas & Electric Power in Nontechnical Language
by Ann Chambers
258 pages, hardcover
$64.95 US/CAN
$79.95 Intl
ISBN: 0-87814-761-6

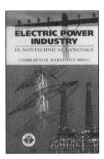

Electric Power Industry in Nontechnical Language
by Denise Warkentin
239 pages, hardcover
$64.95 US/CAN
$79.95 Intl
ISBN: 0-87814-719-5

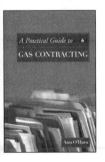

A Practical Guide to Gas Contracting
by Ann O'Hara
467 pages, hardcover
$64.95 US/CAN
$79.95 Intl
ISBN: 0-87814-764-0

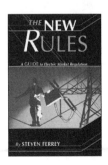

The New Rules: A Guide to Electric Market Regulation
by Steven Ferrey
370 pages, hardcover
$64.95 US/CAN
$79.95 Intl
ISBN: 0-87814-790-X

To purchase a PennWell book...

- Visit our online store www.pennwell-store.com, or
- Call 1.800.752.9764 (US) or +1.918.831.9421 (Intl), or
- Fax 1.877.218.1348 (US) or +1.918.831.9555 (Intl)